A

BRIEF VIE

OF THE

𝔥𝔢𝔞𝔳𝔢𝔫𝔩𝔶 𝔇𝔬𝔠𝔱𝔯𝔦𝔫𝔢𝔰,

CONCERNING

MARRIAGE,

THE

𝔏𝔦𝔣𝔢 𝔬𝔣 𝔐𝔞𝔫 𝔞𝔣𝔱𝔢𝔯 𝔇𝔢𝔞𝔱𝔥,

AND

THE SECOND ADVENT:

COMPILED FROM THE WRITINGS OF

THE HONOURABLE E. SWEDENBORG.

"If any man will do His will, he shall know of the doctrine, whether it be of God, or whether I speak of myself." JOHN vii. 17.

EDINBURGH:

PUBLISHED BY JOHN ANDERSON, JUN., AND JAMES ROBERTSON EDINBURGH; ROBERTSON & ATKINSON, GLASGOW; D. PEAT PERTH; JAMES ADAM, DUNDEE; W. TROUP, ABERDEEN; W. & W. CLARKE, MANCHESTER; SIMPKIN & MARSHALL, SHERWOOD, GILBERT,& PIPER, J.S. HODSON, AND T. GOYDER, LONDON.

MDCCCXXVIII.

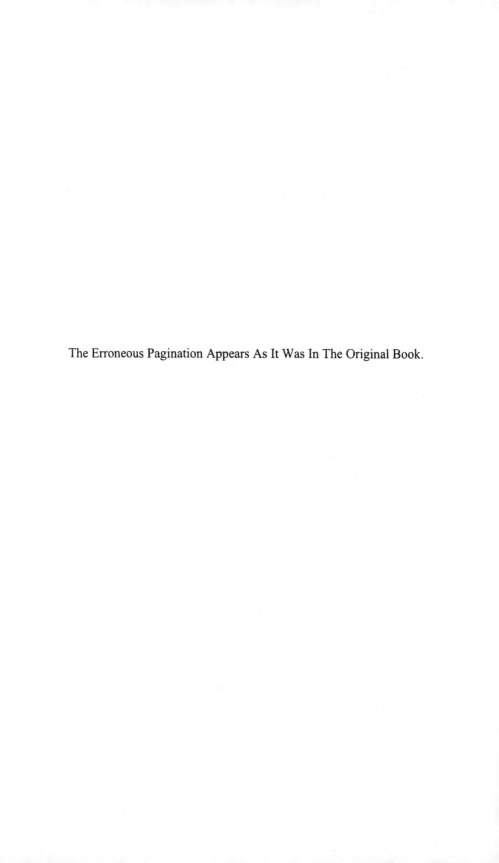

The Erroneous Pagination Appears As It Was In The Original Book.

PREFACE.

THE religious public is here presented with a clear and concise view of what that extraordinary man—Emanuel Swedenborg, has written on three of as deeply interesting subjects as can well be imagined, viz. MARRIAGE, THE LIFE OF MAN AFTER DEATH, AND THE SECOND ADVENT OF THE LORD; respecting all of which, it is lamentable to say, the grossest ignorance prevails. The object, therefore, of this pnblication is, that they may be understood in their true light, and also that this knowledge may be communicated with even better effect, than by means of the voluminous works from which it is collated.

Let it not, however, be supposed, that this "compilation" is either calculated or intended to give a *better* explanation of those subjects, than is to be met with in Swedenborg's own works; on the contrary, from its very nature, it can neither give so full nor so perfect an idea of them. And yet we trust, that enough is said to convince every sincere and devout enquirer after truth, that the explanation given

of them is perfectly consistent both with the Sacred
Scriptures and sound reason. But should any difficulty occur on any particular point, the reader is re-
quested to bear in mind that, as this is but an Abridg-
ment, he cannot expect to find every thing so clearly stated as in the works themselves; which we
hope, for his own sake, he will be led to examine,
not doubting but if he only does so in a right spirit,
he will find every thing cleared up to his entire satisfaction.

The only apprehension is, that he may, like many
others, be prevented from perusing them, from an
idea that the Author was an impostor, or at least
an enthusiast, on account of his spiritual communications. Just as if this great man had been induced
to fabricate such stories, merely with the view of
making people more readily receive the doctrines
which he taught, when he must have known it
was calculated to have quite the contrary effect!

That the reader, however, should not be deterred
by such prejudice, from examining the works, it may
be sufficient to remark, that the *possibility* of what
the Author asserts, as to his spiritual communications, is not to be disputed : many instances of a

similar nature being recorded in the Sacred Scriptures. But a still stronger and more convincing argument is, that the doctrines which the heaven-taught Swedenborg was the honoured instrument of promulgating, especially those on which the salvation of man more immediately depends, have nothing whatever to do, either with the truth or falsehood of his spiritual communications, but rest entirely for their support and confirmation on the evidence which he adduces from the Sacred Scriptures. All that is asked is, that the Author and his works may be fairly tried by the Divine rule—" *To the law and to the testimony: if they speak not according to this Word, it is because there is no light in them.*" Isa. viii. 20.

But let us hear what the Honourable Author himself says on this interesting subject:

" I am aware, that many who read what I have related, con-
" cerning the spiritual world, will believe that they are fictions
" of the imagination; but I protest in truth, that they are not
" fictions, but were truly seen and heard; not seen in any state
" of the mind asleep, but in a state of full wakefulness; for it
" hath pleased the Lord to manifest himself to me, and to send
" me to teach the things relative to the New Church, which is
" meant by the NEW JERUSALEM in the Revelation; for which

" purpose he hath opened the interiors of my mind and spirit, by
" virtue of which privilege, it hath been granted me to be in the
" spiritual world with angels, and at the same time in the natu-
" ral world with men, and this now for twenty-five years. For
" who in the Christian orb would have known any thing con-
" cerning heaven, and concerning the joys and the happiness
" therein experienced, the science whereof is a science of sal-
" vation, unless it had pleased the Lord to open to some person
" or other the sight of his spirit, and to shew and teach? That
" similar things exist in the spiritual world, is very manifest
" from what was seen and heard by the apostle John, as des-
" cribed in the Apocalypse,—as that he saw the Son of Man in
" the midst of seven candlesticks, and also a tabernacle, temple,
" ark, and altar in heaven; a book sealed with seven seals, the
" book opened, and horses going forth thence; four animals
" around the throne; twelve thousand chosen out of each
" tribe; locusts ascending out of the abyss; a dragon, and his
" combat with Michael; a woman bringing forth a male child,
" and flying into a wilderness by reason of the dragon; two
" beasts, one ascending out of the sea, the other out of the
" earth; a woman sitting upon a scarlet beast; the dragon cast
" out into a lake of fire and sulphur; a white horse, and a
" great supper; a new heaven and a new earth, and the holy
" Jerusalem descending, described as to its gates, wall, and
" foundation; also a river of water of life, and trees of life
" yielding fruits every month; besides several other particulars,
" all which things were seen by John, and were seen, whilst,
" as to his spirit, he was in the spiritual world and in hea-
" ven. Not to mention the things seen by the apostles after
" the Lord's resurrection; and what were afterwards seen and

" heard by Peter, Acts xi., and also by Paul; moreover, by
" the prophets, as by Ezekiel, in that he saw four animals,
" which were cherubs, chap. i. and chap. x.; a new temple
" and a new earth, and an angel measuring them, chap. xl. to
" xlviii.; that he was led away to Jerusalem, and saw there a-
" bominations: and also into Chaldea into captivity, chap. viii.
" and chap. xi. The case was similar with Zechariah, in
" that he saw a man riding between myrtles, chap. i. 8. and
" following verses; that he saw four horns, and afterwards a
" man with a measuring-line in his hand, chap. iii. 1. and fol-
" lowing verses; that he saw a candlestick and two olives, chap.
" iv. 2. and following veres; that he saw a flying roll, and an
" ephah, chap. v. 1, 6.; that he saw four chariots going forth
" between two mountains, and horses, chap. vi. 1. and following
" verses. So likewise with Daniel, in that he saw four beasts
" coming up out of the sea, chap. viii. 1. and following verses;
" also combats of a ram and he-goat, chap. viii. 1. and following
" verses; that he saw the angel Gabriel, and had much dis-
" course with him, chap. ix. That the servant of Elisha saw
" chariots and horses of fire round about Elisha, and that he
" saw them when his eyes were open, 2 Kings vi. 17. From
" these, and several other instances in the Word, it is evident,
" that the things which exist in the spiritual world, appeared to
" many both before and after the Lord's coming: what wonder
" then is it, that the same things should now also appear at
" the commencement of the Church, or when the New Je-
" rusalem is coming down from the Lord out of heaven?"

On the mind of any one at all acquainted with
the private character of this great and good man, or

with the estimation in which he was universally held (by those who knew him personally,) for his talents and learning, but more especially for his exemplary piety, and unassuming simplicity of manners, the above declaration, coming from such a person, cannot fail to make a powerful impression ; but as few comparatively have even so much as heard of such a person, or what little they may have heard, being very possibly more to his prejudice than otherwise, we would earnestly recommend for the information of such, a small work, entitled, " *An Account of Emanuel Swedenborg, as contained in an Eulogium to his Memory, by M. Sandel :*" commonly known as an oration delivered in the Swedish Royal Academy of Sciences, on occasion of Swedenborg's death, by the Chevalier de Sandel, Superintendant of the Mines, and Knight of the Order of the Polar Star, at a meeting of the Academy held in the Great Hall of the House of Nobles, Oct. 7th, 1772. The reader, however, will be able to form some idea both of his public and private character, from the following extracts :—

" Permit me," says M. de Sandel, to the noblemen and gentlemen around him, " to entertain you this day upon a subject which is intended to revive the agreeable remembrance of a man celebrated for his virtues and his knowledge, one of the oldest members of this Academy, and one whom we all knew and loved. The sentiments of esteem and friendship with which we all regarded the late Emanuel Swedenborg, assure me of the pleasure with which you will listen to me, while he is the subject of my discourse: happy should I be, could I answer your expectations, and draw his eulogium in the manner it deserves!"

"Represent to yourselves in Swedenborg the following happy assemblage of qualities: An excellent memory, a penetrating understanding, a quick conception, and the soundest judgment, united to an insatiable and ardent desire for making the most profound attainments in Philosophy, in all the branches of Mathematics, in Natural History, in Mechanics, in Anatomy, and finally, in Theology; not to mention the Oriental and European languages, in which he was well versed. Observe in him, well formed habits, acting in concert with the dictates of reason, especially in regard to the admirable order in which he always arranged his ideas. Add to all this, the best heart and the best character; which are evidenced by the rules he laid down for the government of his own thoughts and conduct, as I have found them noted in various parts of his manuscripts. They are as follows: 'I. To read often, and meditate well 'upon the Word of God. II. To be always resigned and con-'tented under the various dispensations of Divine Providence. 'III. To observe always a propriety of behaviour, and to keep 'the conscience clear and void of offence. IV. To obey what 'is ordained; to discharge with fidelity the duties of one's em-'ployment; and to do every thing that depends on one's self, 'to be useful to all without exception.'—Behold here the pic-

ture of Swedenborg's inward state of mind ! None but such as
are blinded by prejudice, can either think or say that it is not a
true likeness, or can fail to recognize in it the man himself."

" I have, perhaps, said too much on Swedenborg's writings
on spiritual subjects, as these are not matters proper to be dis-
cussed in an Academy of Sciences. Suffice it then to add, that
the good qualities, the talents, and the merit of this Author,
shine with brilliancy, even where we look in him for weak-
nesses inseparable from human nature. If his desire of knowledge went too far, it at least evinces in him an ardent desire to
obtain information himself, and to convey it to others; for you
never find in him any mark of pride, or conceit, of rashness, or
of intention to deceive. And if he is not to be numbered
among the doctors of the church, he at least holds an honourable rank among sublime moralists, and deserves to be in-
stanced as a pattern of virtue, and of respect for his Creator."

" He was a sincere friend of mankind."

" In company, he was cheerful and agreeable. By way of re-
laxation, amid his constant labours, he sought the conversation
of men of intelligence, by whom he was always well received,
and highly respected. As a public functionary, he was upright
and just;—while he discharged his duties with great exactness,
he neglected nothing but his own advancement."

" As a member of the Equestrian Order of the House of Nobles, he took his seat in several Diets; in which capacity his
conduct was always irreproachable. He lived under the reigns
of many of our sovereigns, and enjoyed the particular favour
and kindness of them all."

" Swedenborg (and this I mention without intending to make
a merit of it) was never married. This was not however owing to
any indifference towards the sex; for he esteemed the compa-

ny of a fine and intelligent woman as one of the most agreeable of pleasures; but his profound studies rendered expedient for him the quiet of a single life. It may be truly said, that he was solitary, but never sad. He enjoyed such excellent health, that he scarcely ever experienced the least indisposition. Always filled with an inward content, he, under all circumstances, possessed his soul in peace; and he led a life in the highest degree happy, till the moment that nature demanded her rights. He died in London, on the 29th of March in the present year [1772] in the eighty-fifth year of his age."

Another striking testimony in respect to the character of Swedenborg, is that of Count Hopkin, one of the institutors of the Swedish Royal Academy of Sciences, which, being a man of eminent learning, he served for a considerable period in the quality of Secretary. He afterwards was, for many years, prime minister of the kingdom; and only died in 1790. In a letter to his friend General Tuxen of Elsinore, he writes as follows: "All I could say," states the Count, "by way of preliminary on this subject, regards the person of the late Assessor Swedenborg. I have not only known him for these two and forty years, but also, some time since, daily frequented his company. A man, who, like me, has lived long in the world, and even in an extensive career of life, must have had numerous opportunities of knowing men as to their virtues and vices: but I

do not recollect ever to have known a man of more
uniformly virtuous character than Swedenborg. He
was always contented, and never fretful and morose,
although throughout his life, his soul was occupied
with sublime thoughts and speculations. He was
a true philosopher, and lived like one. He was
gifted with a most happy genius, and a fitness for
every science; which made him shine in all that he
pursued. I once represented to this venerable man,
in rather a serious manner, that he would do better not to mix his beautiful writings with so many
revelations, which ignorance makes a jest of, and
turns into ridicule. But he answered, ' that this
did not depend on himself: that he was too old to
trifle with spiritual things, and too much concerned
for his eternal happiness, to give into such notions
were they unfounded.' When the generality are
speaking of the theology of Swedenborg, they always dwell on his revelations, and think that every
thing consists in these. Few persons have judi-
ciously read his works, which every where sparkle
with genius. The Swedenborgian system is more
comprehensible to our reason, and less complicated,
than other systems; and while it forms virtuous
men and good citizens, it prevents all kinds of enthu-

siasm and superstition, both of which occasion so many and such cruel vexations, or ridiculous singularities in the world."

The above testimony must surely be allowed to carry the greatest weight, both as it refers to the character of Swedenborg himself, and of his writings.

Dr Gabriel Andrew Beyer, Professor of Greek Literature, and Assessor in the Consistory of Gottenburgh, became one of Swedenborg's most intimate friends, and one of the most active promoters of his sentiments. This drew upon him a severe persecution from the Consistory. The matter was carried before the supreme government, when, in compliance with an order from the king, Dr Beyer presented to his majesty, Jan. 2, 1770, a declaration of his sentiments in regard to the doctrines of Swedenborg. Towards the close, the amiable and learned Author expresses himself thus: " In obedience to your majesty's most gracious command, that I should deliver a full and positive declaration respecting the writings of Swedenborg, I do acknowledge it to be my duty to declare in all humble confidence, that, so far as I have proceeded in the study of them, and according to such gifts for investigation and judgment as I possess, I have found in them nothing but what closely coincides with the words of the Lord Himself; and that they shine with a light truly divine."

But beside his own countrymen, and other foreigners, some who knew him in this country have added their most decided suffrage to his excellent qualities.

Of these, the principal is the Rev. Thomas Hartley, M. A. Rector of Winwick in Northamptonshire; who having met with some of Swedenborg's works, sought an acquaintance with their author, and was admitted by him to his intimate friendship. Mr Hartley has left his testimony respecting him on record, in the Prefaces to the English editions of the works " On the Intercourse between the Soul and the Body," and "On Heaven and Hell," and in a letter to the translator of the " True Christian Religion," inserted in the preface to that work. In the first of these prefaces, Mr H. says, respecting his author, " I have conversed with him at different times, and in company with a gentleman of a learned profession, and of extensive intellectual abilities: we have had confirmation of these things from his own mouth, and have received his testimony, and do both of us consider, this our acquaintance with the author and his writings among the greatest blessings of our lives." " The extensive learning displayed in his writings evinces him to be the scholar and the philosopher; and his polite behaviour and address bespeak him the gentleman. He affects no honour, but declines it; pursues no worldly interest, but spends his substance in travelling and printing, in order to communicate instruction to mankind : and he is so far from the ambition of heading a sect, that wherever he resides on his travels he is a mere solitary and almost inaccessible, though in his own country of a free and open behaviour. He has nothing of the precision in his manner, nothing of melancholy in his temper, and nothing in the least bordering on the enthusiast in his conversation and writings." Mr H. makes similar remarks in his letter to the translator of the True Christian Religion : " The great Swedenborg was a man of uncommon humility." " He was of a catholic spirit, and loved all good men of every church, making at the same time all candid allowance for the innocence of involuntary error." " However self-denying in his own person, as to gratifications and indulgences, even within the

bounds of moderation; yet nothing severe, nothing of the precision appeared in him, but on the
contrary, an inward serenity and complacency of
mind were manifest in the sweetness of his looks
and outward demeanour."—"It may reasonably
be supposed, that I have weighed the character
of our illustrious author in the scale of my
best judgment, from the personal knowledge I had
of him, from the best information I could procure
respecting him, and from a diligent perusal of his
writings: and according thereto, I have found him
to be the sound divine, the good man, the deep philosopher, the universal scholar, and the polite gentleman: and I further believe, that he had a high
degree of illumination from the Spirit of God; was
commissioned by Him as an extraordinary messen-
ger to the world; and had communication with angels and the spiritual world, far beyond any since
the time of the apostles. As such, I offer his character to the world, solemnly declaring, that to the
best of my knowledge, I am not herein led by any
partiality or private views whatever, being much
dead to every worldly interest, and accounting myself as unworthy of any higher character than that
of a penitent sinner."—What Mr Hartly here

says of himself, is unquestionably true : for he was well known to many of the religious characters of that day, as a man of the deepest piety, and he was at this time (in 1781,) very far advanced in years, and near the end of his earthly career ; to the testimony of such a man to the character of Swedenborg, what exception can be made ?

The " gentleman of a learned profession, and of extensive intellectual abilities," mentioned by M r Hartley above, was the late Dr Messiter, an eminent physician of that time. What his opinion of Swedenborg, the result of personal acquaintance, was, appears from his correspondence with the Professors of Divinity, at Edinburgh, Glasgow, and Aberdeen ; (see Intellectual Repository, vol. iii. *(first series)* p. 449, &c.) to which Universities, by desire of Swedenborg, he, in 1769, presented some of his works. In his letter to Dr Hamilton at Edinburgh, Dr M. says, " As I have had the honour of being frequently admitted to the author's company when he was in London, and to converse with him on various points of learning, I will venture to affirm, that there are no parts of mathematical, philosophical, or medical knowledge, nay, I

b

believe I might justly say, of human literature, to
which he is in the least a stranger; yet so totally
insensible is he of his own merit, that I am confi-
dent he does not know that he has any; and, as
himself somewhere says of the angels, he always
turns his head away on the slightest encomium.
(Dr Hamilton, in his answer, candidly says, "I
have seen enough to convince me that the Honourable Author is a very learned and pious man; qualities that shall ever command my respect.") So,
in his letter to Dr Gerard at Aberdeen, Dr Messiter, speaking of Swedenborg's works, says, "They
are the productions of a man whose good qualities, resulting from his natural and acquired abilities, I can, with much truth, from my frequent
converse with him, assert, are a high ornament to
human nature. Credulity, prejudice, or partiality,
seem to have no share in his composition or character; nor is he in the least influenced by any avaricious or interestded views. A proof of this last
assertion was afforded me, by his refusing an offer
of any money he might have occasion for while in
England; which was made him on a supposal, that
his want of connexions, in a place where he was a

stranger, might prove an obstacle to his divine pursuits."

With the Englishmen whose approbation of Swedenborg's sentiments was strengthened by a personal acquaintance with himself, must be reckoned the late Mr William Cookworthy ; a man of most superior character, the friend of the first Lord Camelford, and of Captain Jervis, afterwards Earl St Vincent, and the associate of many of the literati of his day. This gentleman testified his satisfaction with Swedenborg and his writings, by joining with Mr Hartley in translating the Treatise on Heaven and Hell, and defraying the whole expense of the printing and publishing. (See a Memoir of him in the " Intellectual Repository," *(new series)* vol. i. p. 439, &c.)

In the testimony to Swedenborg's virtues and attainments, thus borne by so many most unexceptionable witnesses, who knew him well, and against which no opposing testimony whatever, from persons acquainted with him, can be adduced, we surely have the most satisfactory confirmation, not only as to his exemplary life and character, but as to his qualifications for the office to which he declares he was appointed, namely, to communicate the truths connected with the second advent of the Lord, on the supposition that the time for that event has arrived. We also see that many men of the very first respectability, intelligence, and learning, who formed their opinion from a knowledge of the man as well as his writings, believed, during his life time, that he actually was the Instrument appointed for that purpose; not to mention the thousands, in the present day, of all ranks, and in almost all countries, who conscientiously believe the same thing.

With respect to the following work, it is given almost entirely in the very words of Swedenborg, and the little which is drawn from other sources, independent of what is specified, is so much in unison with his writings, that it was thought unnecessary to make any distinction between them. The compiler's object was, to give the whole in a connected series, and only to introduce what was absolutely necessary to preserve such connection. And having now done his best, he leaves the result with HIM under whose divine auspices, he trusts, it has been begun, continued, and ended. Amen.

AN ANSWER TO A LETTER FROM A FRIEND,

By the Author.

London, 1769.

I TAKE pleasure in the friendship you express for me in your Letter, and return you thanks for the same; but as to the praises which you bestow upon me, I only receive them as tokens of your love of the truths contained in my writings, and so refer them to the Lord our Saviour, from whom is the all of truth, because He is THE TRUTH (John xiv. 6.). It is the concluding part of your Letter that chiefly engages my attention, where you say as follows : ' As after your de-
' parture from England, disputes may arise on the subject of your
' writings, and so give occasion to defend their author against such
' false reports and aspersions, as they who are no friends to truth may
' invent to the prejudice of his character, may it not be of use, in
' order to refute any calumnies of that kind, that you leave in my
' hands some short account of yourself, as concerning, for example,
' your degrees in the university, the offices you have borne, your
' family and connexions, the honours which I am told have been con-
' ferred upon you, and such other particulars as may serve to the vin-
' dication of your character, if attacked : that so any ill-grounded pre-
' judices may be obviated or removed ? For where the honour and
' interest of truth are concerned, it certainly behoves us to employ
' all lawful means in its defence and support.' After reflecting on the foregoing passage, I was induced to comply with your friendly advice, by briefly communicating the following circumstances of my life.

I was born at Stockholm, in the year of our Lord 1689, Jan. 29th. My Father's name was Jasper Swedberg, who was Bishop of Westrogothia, and of celebrated character in his time. He was also elected a member of the English Society for the propagation of the Gospel, and appointed as Bishop over the Swedish Churches in Pensylvania and London, by King Charles XII. In the year 1710 I began my travels, first into England, and afterwards into Holland, France, and Germany, and returned home in 1714. In the year 1716, and afterwards, I frequently conversed with Charles XII. King of Sweden, who was pleased to bestow on me a large share of his favour, and in that year appointed me to the office of Assessor in the Metalic College, in which office I continued from that time till the year 1747, when I quitted the office, but still retained the salary annexed to it, as an appointment for life. The sole reason of my withdrawing from the business of that employment was, that I might be more at liberty to apply myself to that new function to which the Lord had called me. A higher degree of rank was then offered me, which I declined to accept, lest pride on account of it should enter my mind. In 1719 I was enobled by Queen Ulrica Eleonora, and named *Swedenborg*; from which time I have taken my seat with the Nobles of the Equestrian Order, in the Triennial Assemblies of the States. I am a Fellow, by invitation, of the Royal Academy of Sciences at Stockholm, but have never sought admission into any other literary society, as I belong to an angelical society, in which things relating to heaven and the soul are the only subjects of discourse and entertainment ; whereas in our literary societies the attention is wholly taken up with things relating to the world and the body. In the year 1734 I published the *Regnum Minerale*, at Leipsic, in three volumes, folio; and in 1738 I took a journey into Italy, and staid a year at Venice and Rome.

With respect to my family connexions: I had four sisters; one of them was married to Erick Benzelius, afterwards promoted to the Archbishoprick of Upsal; and thus I became related to the two succeeding Archbishops of that see, both named Benzelius, and younger brothers of the former. My second sister was married to Lars Benzelstierna, who was promoted to a provincial government: but these are both dead: however, two bishops who are related to me are still living; one of them is named Filenius, Bishop of Ostrogothia, who now officiates as President of the Ecclesiastical Order in the Diet at Stockholm, in the room of the Archbishop who is infirm: he married the daughter of my sister; the other who is named Benzelstierna, Bishop of Westermannia and Dalecarlia, is the son of my second sister; not to mention others of my family who are dignified. I converse freely, and am in friendship, with all the Bishops of my country, who are ten in number, and also with the sixteen Senators, and the rest of the Grandees who love and honour me, as knowing that I am in fellowship with angels. The King and Queen themselves, and also the three Princes their sons, show me all kind countenance; and I was once invited to eat with the King and Queen at their table, (an honour granted only to the Peers of the realm,) and likewise since with the hereditary prince. All in my own country wish for my return home; so far am I from having the least fear of being persecuted there, as you seem to apprehend, and are also kindly solicitous to provide against; and should any thing of that kind befal me elsewhere it will give me no concern.

Whatever of worldly honour and advantage may appear to be in the things before-mentioned, I hold them as matters of respectively little moment, because what is far better, I have been called to a holy office by the Lord himself, who most graciously manifested Himself in person to me His servant, in the year 1743, and then opened my sight into the spiritual world, and endowed me with the gift of conversing with spirits and angels, which has been continued to me to this day. From that time I began to print and publish various *arcana*, that have been either seen by me or revealed to me; as concerning heaven and hell; the state of men after death; the true worship of God; the spiritual sense of the Word, and many other most important matters tending to salvation and true wisdom; and the only motive which has induced me at different times to leave my home and visit foreign countries, was the desire of being useful, and of communicating the arcana entrusted to me. As to this world's wealth, I have sufficient, and more I neither ask nor wish for.

Your letter has drawn the mention of these things from me with a view, as you suggest, that any ill-grounded prejudices may be removed. Farewell; and from my heart I wish you all felicity both in this world and in the next, which I make no doubt of your obtaining if you look and pray to our Lord.

EMAN. SWEDENBORG.

CONTENTS.

ON MARRIAGE.

b 2

CONTENTS.

ON MARRIAGE.

SECTION I.

INTRODUCTION.

" How sweet the charms of wedded love,
When souls unite with views sincere!
The hallow'd bands are fix'd above,
And Heaven protects the constant pair.

" Theirs is the soft, the spotless flame,
That ceaseless wakes the chaste desire;
Their tranquil bliss still flows the same,
And Love and Truth their hearts inspire."

MARRIAGES, it must be admitted, when entered
into, merely from natural or external motives, without regard to agreement of minds, are not in reality
marriages, but only the *appearance* of them, which,
in consequence of the want of spiritual affinity between the parties, must necessarily be dissolved, if
not in this life, at all events in the future, where
minds alone love and are beloved. But when, on
the other hand, they are contracted from a sincere
and mutual affection, or more correctly, from a
desire of being united first as to *minds*, and thence as
to *bodies*, (a sure proof the parties are principled in

love truly conjugial,*) they are then, and only then,
such as "God hath joined together," or such as
are effected in heaven, and consequently indissoluble.
For whether we speak of being married as to minds,
or married in heaven, it is the same thing; as the
minds of those who are principled in love truly conjugial, (which is only another name for true religion,) are actually in heaven, or, what amounts
to the same, have heaven in them, in consequence
of that very love itself being heaven.   Accordingly
we find both heaven and the church compared in
the Word to *a marriage ;* and hence, whether we
speak of being in the heavenly marriage, or principled in conjugial love, it also amounts to the same,
inasmuch as it is this love which properly constitutes both heaven and the church in man.

From a work lately published (*" An Appeal in
Behalf of the Views of the Eternal World and State,"
by the Rev. S. Noble,*) we select the following extracts, in further illustration of the subject :

"Among the symptoms of corruption of manners
and grossness of sentiment, which are so general in
the present day, there is none more conspicuous and
glaring, than the low ideas which are almost every
where met with, of the nature and obligation of the
conjugial covenant.   Who thinks that the true love of
marriage is essentially holy, and the love of all connections alien therefrom is essentially profane?   Who

---

* The term *conjugial* is here used, instead of *conjugal*, as more
expressive, from its origin, of a real marriage-union.

regards the difference between them as intrinsically inherent in the things themselves, independently of all merely arbitrary appointment? How many are there in fact, who look upon marriage as but a sort of legalized adultery, and upon adultery as differing in nothing but the want of the legal sanction of marriage! Hence, among the topics of revilement brought forward against the doctrines of the New Jerusalem, none is more frequently insisted on, none is more confided in, as capable of exposing them to utter derision and contempt than this—that they affirm true marriage to be a permanent institution, true marriages to be indissoluble, even by the power of the grave; and that in regard to all who enter the heavenly kingdom, should circumstances have prevented them from finding proper partners here, they will find such there, with whom their union continually becomes more perfect, and fraught with true delight through eternity."

"The difference between the male and female exists quite as decidedly in their minds, as in their outward forms, so that if it were possible to abolish all difference in the shape of their persons, this would, by no means, be sufficient to abolish all real distinction of sex; the sex is in the mind also, and can never be extirpated thence. On every subject whatsoever, one part of the species will ever think and feel as men, and the other as women. The minds, it is true, both of men and women, are constituted both of will and intellect, affection and intelligence: but who does not see that the man takes

his distinguishing character from the predominating
strength of his intellect, and woman hers from the
predominating strength of her affections? Great
disputes have been agitated on the question, Whether there is an inferiority on the part of females,
compared with men: but as unfortunately, both
parties have looked on intellect as the distinguishing
faculty of the human race, and have overlooked,
as of minor importance, the no less essential and
valuable attributes of will and affection, men, in asserting their pre-eminence, have relied on the former alone; and female writers, with some auxiliary
males, in denying the superiority, have allowed the
principle for which it is claimed, to be the right
criterion of it; and hence, instead of making good
their claim, as they might have done, had they only
asserted a general equality, have failed, through
claiming an equality in the same principle of intellect.

" Intellect is not a more excellent attribute than
affection; and in affection, undoubtedly, the superiority is all on the side of the female sex.   And the
sexes were thus endowed with equal, but distinct
excellences, that they might not engage in rivalry,
but combine in union: that female affection might
both soften and exalt the intellect of the male, and
that masculine intellect might guide and protect female affection.   Affection without intellect is blind;
intellect without affection is dead: when united, intellect is quickened with life, affection rejoices in
light.   The female mind, however, is by no means

destitute of intellect, nor the male destitute of affection: but who can look at both, and not allow, that the two principles exist in each in unequal proportions, so that one, only, forms the predominating characteristic of each? Hence it is, that when a male and female mind really enter into interior union, which never can take place, but when both are in the heavenly marriage of goodness and truth, the perfection of each is immensely exalted, and with it the happiness; each is a more perfect angel than either could be separately; and the union of minds becomes so perfect, that before the Lord, by whom minds only are looked at, they become a one."

" By male and female in a purely spiritual sense, are meant the principles of intellect and will as formed for the reception of truth and good respectively; the eternal law of order and of God respecting which is, they should be united, and never be separated by the self-derived intelligence of man; which is what the Lord means when He says, "What God hath joined together let not man put asunder." If therefore the minds of a male and female are in the heavenly marriage of goodness and truth, it follows that they must be united in pairs, in a marriage expressive of that within."

In agreement with the above remarks, it is taught and believed in the New Church, that true and genuine marriage is one and the same with regeneration, inasmuch as the union of will and under-

standing, or rather of good and truth therein implanted by the Lord, (in which regeneration solely
consists,) is not capable of being fully effected but
by the spiritual marriage of a male and female,
whether they may have been externally married in
the world or not. Thus we are instructed, that
man is not regenerated alone, no more than he was
originally created alone, but that a male and female
are always regenerated together. This is also confirmed by the Apostle, where he says, " The man
is not without the woman, neither is the woman
without the man, *in the Lord.*" 1 Cor. xi. 11. And
the reason is, because the male was created to be
the understanding of truth, thus truth in form,
and the female was created to be the will of good,
thus good in form ; and there is implanted in each
from there inmost principle, an inclination to conjunction into one : hence it is, that regeneration or
the union of good and truth in the mind, cannot be
complete, but by the union of two minds into one.
If, indeed, a male and female were not to be so united, it is evident that each would only be a half or
divided man ; whereas by spiritual marriage, " they
twain" become, in conformity with the Divine command, " one flesh," or one full and complete man,
an *image and likeness of God.*

It is further taught, that by marriage in a higher
or more extensive sense, is to be understood the conjunction of the Lord and the church, from which the
origin of spiritual marriage is derived and exists in

the minds of two, in whom or between whom
is the marriage of good and truth; for the Lord
with such enters by influx into their minds with
the good of love, whilst they receive Him, or the
good of His love, in truths, and that thus the
Lord is in man and man in the Lord. So far, therefore, as the truths appertaining to man are conjoined
to good, so far man is conjoined to the Lord and to
heaven: hence then is the very origin itself of conjugial love, wherefore it is the very plane itself of
the divine influx: hence it is that the conjunction
of good and truth in the heavens, is called the heavenly marriage, and that heaven, in the Word, is
compared to a marriage, and is also called a marriage, and that the Lord is called the Bridegroom and
Husband, and heaven, with the church, the Bride,
and also the Wife.

From what hath been now said concerning the
origin of conjugial love, it may be concluded who
are principled in that love, and who are not; that
they are principled in conjugial love who are in
divine good from divine truths; and that conjugial
love is so far genuine, as the truths which are conjoined to good are more genuine: and whereas all
good, which is conjoined to truths, is from the Lord
God the Saviour, it follows, that no one can be in
love truly conjugial, unless he acknowledges Him as
God and Divine, even as to His Humanity, for without that acknowledgement the Lord cannot flow-in,
and be conjoined to the truths appertaining to man.

Lastly it is taught, that by Marriage, in the supreme sense, is to be understood the union of the Lord's Divinity with His Humanity, or what amounts to the same, of the Divine Good with the Divine Truth, which the Lord fully accomplished in Himself during His abode in the world, when He underwent a process of Glorification similar or corresponding to that of man's regeneration, whereby He put off whatever of imperfection belonging to our nature, He had derived from Mary, and put on, at the same time, a DIVINE HUMANITY from the Father—His *internal* Divinity, which was truly the SON OF GOD; in like manner as man, in the process of regeneration, puts off the *old man*, which he derives hereditarily from his parents, and puts on the *new man* which he derives from God, with this difference, that man is made *regenerate* only as to his *spirit*, whereas the Lord was made *Divine* even as to His *Body;* and that thus the Divine Truth or Humanity, called the SON, was fully united or made one with the Divine Good or Divinity, called the FATHER, agreeably to the Lord's own words,—" I AND THE FATHER ARE ONE."

SECTION II.

SHEWING how Marriage, in a spiritual sense, is one and the same with Regeneration.

" The kingdom of heaven is likened unto a marriage." MATT. xxii. 2.

THAT marriage, in a spiritual sense, is one and the same with regeneration, or, in other words, that to be regenerated is to be spiritually married, is a truth which could never have been discovered from human reason alone, no, nor even from the WORD—the Divine Source of all truth—unaided by the light of heaven; but when once the mind is so enlightened, it may be clearly seen and confirmed from the Divine Word, particularly in the history of the creation of Adam and his wife Eve, which it will be found is nothing else but an historical description of man's spiritual creation or regeneration.

The prayer of the inspired Psalmist, on this occasion, should not be forgotten,—" *Open Thou mine eyes, that I may behold wondrous things out of THY LAW.*" Also, that it is written,—" *Then opened He their understanding, that they might understand the SCRIPTURES.*

That at creation, there was implanted in the man and woman an inclination and also faculty of con-

A 2

junction into one, and that both this inclination
and faculty are still in man and woman, is evident
from the book of creation, and at the same time
from the Lord's words : In the book of creation called GENESIS, it is written, "And the rib which
Jehovah God had taken from the man, built He
into a woman, and brought her unto the man.   And
the man said, This now is bone of my bones, and
flesh of my flesh; she shall be called woman, because she was taken out of man: therefore shall a
man leave his father and his mother, and shall cleave
to his wife, and THEY SHALL BE ONE FLESH," chap.
ii. 22, 23, 24.   The Lord also spake like words
in Matthew, " Have ye not read that He who made
them from the beginning, made them male and female, and said, For this cause shall a man leave father and mother, and cleave unto his wife, and THEY
TWAIN SHALL BE ONE FLESH? WHEREFORE THEY
ARE NO MORE TWAIN BUT ONE FLESH," chap. xix.
4, 5.   From these words it is evident, that the
woman was created out of the man, and that each
hath an inclination and faculty to re-unite themselves into one; that such re-union means into
one man or one mind, is also manifest from the
book of creation, where both together are called
man, for it is written, " In the day that God created man, He created them male and female, and
called their name man," chap. v. 2.; it is there written, He called their name Adam, but Adam and
man are one expression in the Hebrew tongue.

Moreover, both together are called man in the same
book, chap. i. 27.; iii. 22, 23, 24. By one flesh
is also signified one man, as is evident from these
passages in the Word, where mention is made of all
flesh, by which is signified every man, as Gen. vi.
12, 13, 17, 19. Isa. xl. 5, 6.; xlix. 26.; lxvi. 16,
23, 24. Jer. xxv. 31.; xxxii. 27.; xlv. 5. Ezek.
xx. 48.; xxi. 4, 5.; and in other passages. But
what is meant by man's rib, which was formed into
a woman; what by flesh which was closed up in the
place thereof, and thus what by bone of my bones,
and flesh of my flesh; and what by father and mother, whom a man shall leave after marriage; and
what by cleaving to a wife, hath been shewn in the
ARCANA CŒLESTIA, in which work the two books,
Genesis and Exodus, are explained as to the spiritual sense. That by rib is not meant rib, nor by
flesh, flesh, nor by bone, bone, nor by cleaving to,
cleaving to, but that spiritual things are understood,
which correspond thereto, and in consequence thereof are signified thereby, is proved in that work:
that spiritual things are understood, which from two
make one man, is manifest from this consideration,
that conjugial love conjoins them, and this love is
spiritual.

That the woman was taken out from the man,
was shewn just now above from the book of creation;
hence it follows, that there is in each sex a faculty
and inclination to join themselves together into one;
for that which is taken out from any thing, derives

and retains its constituent principle, from the principle proper to the thing whence it was taken; and
as this derived principle is homogeneous with that
from which it was derived, it aspires after a re-union;
and when it is re-united, it is as in itself, when it is
in that from whence it came, and *vice versa.* That
there is a faculty of conjunction of the one sex with
the other, or that they are capable of being united, is
universally allowed; and also that there is an inclination to join themselves the one with the other; for
experience supplies sufficient confirmation in both
cases, and this because the male and female were created to be the essential marriage of good and truth;
the man was created to be the understanding of truth,
and the woman to be the affection of good, consequently the man to be truth, and the woman good.
When the understanding of truth, which is with
the man, makes one with the affection of good,
which is with the woman, there is a conjunction of
two minds into one: this conjunction is the spiritual marriage, from which descends conjugial love:
for when two minds are conjoined to be as one
mind, there is between them love, and this love,
which is the love of spiritual marriage, whilst it
descendeth into the body, becomes the love of natural marriage. That this is the case, any one may,
if he be willing, clearly perceive: the married pair,
who interiorly as to their minds love each other
mutually and interchangeably, also love each other
mutually and interchangeably, as to their bodies.

It is well known, that all love descendeth into the body from the affection of the mind, and that without that origin not any love existeth. Now inasmuch as the origin of conjugial love is the marriage of good and truth, which marriage in its essence is heaven, it is manifest that the origin of the love of adultery is the marriage of evil and the false, which in its essence is hell.

Man cannot become the love which is an image or likeness of God, unless by the marriage of good and truth ; for good and truth intimately love each other, and long to be united that they may be one; the reason is, because divine good and divine truth proceed united from the Lord, consequently they must be united in an angel of heaven, and in a man of the church. This unition can by no means be given except by the marriage of two minds into one, for, as was before said, man was created to be the understanding of truth, consequently truth ; and woman was so created, as to be the affection of good, consequently good : in them therefore is given the conjunction of good and truth : for love truly conjugial, which descendeth from that conjunction, is the very essential medium whereby man becometh the love which is an image or a likeness of God : for the married pair who are in love conjugial from the Lord, love each other mutually and interchangeably from the heart; thus from inmost principles; and hence, although they are apparently two, yet they are actually one ; they are two as to bodies, but one as to life : this may

be compared with the eyes, which are two as to
organs, but one as to sight; in like manner with
the ears, which are two as to organs, but one as to
hearing; so also the arms and the feet are two as
to members but one as to use, the arms being one
as to action, and the feet one as to the act of walk-
ing; in like manner the rest of the organs or members of man which are paired together have also
reference to good and truth; the organ or member
which is on the right to good, and that which is on
the left to truth: it is similar with the husband and
his wife, between whom there is love truly conjugial; they are two as to bodies but one as to life;
wherefore also two conjugial partners in heaven are
not called two angels but one.   From these considerations it is evident that man becometh a form
of love, and thence a form of heaven, which is an
image and likeness of God, by marriage; for marriage is an image of heaven, and love truly conjugial an image of the Lord: and adultery is an
image of hell, and the love of adultery an image
of the devil: love conjugial also appeareth in the
spiritual world in form as an angel, and the love of
adultery in form as a devil.   Reader, treasure this
in thy mind, and inquire whether it be true when
thou livest a man-spirit after death, and thou wilt
see.

SECTION III.

SHEWING how the same distinction which exists in the world, as to the formation of the two sexes, must necessarily continue after death.

"The man is not of the woman, but the woman of the man; neither is the man without the woman, nor the woman without the man, in the Lord." 1 Cor. xi. 8, 11.

INASMUCH as man liveth a man after death, and man is male and female, and there is a distinction between the male principle and the female principle, and such a distinction, that the one cannot be changed into the other, it follows, that after death the male liveth a male, and the female a female, each a spiritual man. It is said, that the male principle cannot be changed into the female principle, nor the female into the male, and that therefore after death the male is a male, and the female a female; but whereas it is not known in what the masculine principle essentially consists, and in what the female principle, therefore it may be expedient briefly to explain it. The essential distinction between the two principles is this; in the masculine principle love is inmost, and its covering is wisdom; or, what is the same thing, the masculine principle is love covered (or veiled) with wisdom; whereas in the female principle the wisdom of the male is inmost, and its covering is the loveth ence derived; but this latter love is female (or feminine) love, and is given of the Lord to the wife by the wisdom of the husband, whereas the former love is male (or masculine) love, which is the love of growing wise,* and is given of the Lord to the husband according to the reception of wisdom; from this circumstance it is, that the male is the wisdom of love, and that the female is the love of that wisdom; wherefore from creation there is implanted in each a love of conjunction so as to become one.   That the female principle is derived from the male, or that the woman was taken out of the man, is manifest from these words in Genesis, " Jehovah God took out one of the man's ribs, and

---

* By growing *wise*, or attaining *wisdom*, according to our Author, is not meant a mere progress in *science*, or what is commonly called *knowledge* and *erudition;* for he shews abundantly in his instructive writings, that man may excel in such attainments, and yet be very far from *wisdom*, or being *wise*. But to grow *wise*, according to the sense in which our Author uses the expression, is to apply science, knowledge, and erudition, to the regulation of the life, and the advancement thereof in the purities of heavenly love and charity: or, in other words, to *grow wise* is to become pure and perfect in the love of God and of our neighbour, by living and acting conformably to the dictates of heavenly truth in the understanding.

closed up the flesh in the place thereof, and He builded the rib, which He had taken out of the man, into a woman, and He brought her to the man: and the man said, This is bone of my bones, and flesh of my flesh, hence she shall be called Eve, because she was taken out of man," chap. ii. 21, 22, 23.

From this primitive formation it follows, that by birth the character of the male is intellectual, and that the female character partakes more of the will principle; or, what amounts to the same, that the male is born to the affection of knowing, of understanding, and of growing wise, whereas the female is born to the love of conjoining herself with the affection in the male. And inasmuch as the interiors form the exteriors to their likeness, and the male (or masculine) form is a form of intellect, and the female (or feminine) form is a form of the love of that intellect, it is from this ground that the male and female differ as to the features of the face, the tone of the voice, and the other parts of the body,—the male partaking of harder features, a harsher tone of voice, and a stronger body, moreover of a bearded chin, and in general of a form less beautiful than that of the female; they differ also in their gestures and manners; in a word, they are not exactly similar in a single respect, but still, in every particular appertaining to each, there is a principle tending to conjunction; yea, the male principle, in the male, is male in every part of his body, even the most minute, and also in every idea

B

of thought, and in every spark of his affection ; the same is true of the female principle in the female; and since of consequence the one cannot be changed into the other, it follows, that after death the male is male, and the female is female.

The reason why good and truth in created subjects are according to the form of each, is, because every subject receives influx according to its form ; the conservation of the whole is nothing else but the perpetual influx of divine good and divine truth into forms created from those principles, for thereby subsistence or conservation is perpetual existence or creation.

Whosoever is desirous, from any of the senses, to acquire to himself an idea respecting good, cannot possibly find it without some adject, which exhibits and manifests it; good, without this, is an entity of no name, and this somewhat, whereby it is exhibited and manifested, hath relation to truth ; pronounce the term good only, and say nothing at the same time of this or of that somewhat with which it is conjoined, or define it abstractedly, or without any adject cohering with it, and you will see that it is a mere nothing, and that it becomes something with its adject; and if you examine the subject with discernment, you will perceive that good, without some adject, is a term of no predication, and thence of no relation, of no affection, and of no state, in a word, of no quality. The case is similar in regard to truth, if it be pronounced and heard without its injunct; that its injunct hath relation to good, may be seen by refined reason. But whereas goods are innumerable, and each ascends to its greatest, and descends to its least, as by the steps of a ladder, and also according to its progression, and according to its quality, varies its name; it is difficult for any but the wise to see the relation of good and truth to their objects, and their conjunction in their objects. That, nevertheless, there is not given any good without truth, nor any truth without good, is manifest from common perception, provided it be first acknowledged that all and singular things of the universe have relation to good and truth; and for this reason, viz. that these two principles are in the Lord God the Creator, yea, that they are Himself, for He is essential divine good, and essential divine truth; but this enters more clearly into the perception of the understanding, and thereby into the ideas of thought; if instead of good we say love, and instead of truth we say wisdom; consequently that in the Lord God the Creator there is divine love and divine wisdom, and that these principles are Himself, that is, that He is essential love and essential wisdom; for these two principles are the same thing as good and truth; the reason is, because good hath relation to love, and truth hath relation to wisdom, for love consists of goods, and wisdom of truths.

Since, therefore, the Lord God the Creator is essential love and essential wisdom, and from Him the universe was created, which thence is a work proceeding from Him, it must needs be, that in all and singular the things created, there is somewhat of of good and of truth from Him; for whatsoever is done and proceeds from any one, derives from him a principle similar to what exists in him. That this is the case, reason also may see from the order in which all and singular things of the universe were created, which order is, that one exists for the sake of another, and that thence one depends upon another, as in the case of the links of a chain; for all things are for the sake of the human race, that from it the angelic heaven may exist, through which creation returns to the Creator himself in whom it originated: hence is the conjunction of the created universe with its Creator, and by conjunction everlasting conservation. It is from this ground that good and truth are called universals of creation: that this is the case, is manifest to every one who takes a rational view of the subject; he sees in every created thing somewhat which hath relation to good, and somewhat which hath relation to truth. The ground and reason why all things in the universe have relation to good and truth, and why good is conjoined whith truth, and truth with good, is, because each proceeds from the Lord, and they proceed from Him as one; and whereas these two principles proceed from Him as the Creator, it follows, that they are in the things created. This may be illustrated by heat and light, which proceed from the sun, in that all things appertaining to the earth are derived from these two principles, for they germinate according to their presence, and according to their conjunction : and natural heat corresponds to spiritual heat, which is love, as natural light corresponds to spiritual light, which is wisdom.

That solitary good is not given, nor solitary truth, may be illustrated and at the same time confirmed, by various considerations, as by the following; that there is not given any essence without a form, nor any form without an essence ; for good is an essence or esse, and truth is that by which the essence is formed and the esse exists. Again, in man there is will and understanding; good is of the will, and truth of the understanding, and will alone doeth nothing, but by the understanding, nor doth understanding alone do any thing but from the will. Again, there are two fountains of bodily life in man, the heart and the lungs; the heart cannot produce any sensitive and moving life, without the respiring lungs, neither can the lungs without the heart; the heart hath relation to good, and the respiration of the lungs to truth; there is also a correspondence between them. The same is evident also from the creation of the two sexes, in that they were created for the reception of good and truth, or of love and wisdom from the Lord; the male was created to become wisdom, grounded in the love of growing wise, and the female was created to become the love of the male grounded in his wisdom, and consequent-

ly formed according thereto; from which consideration it is manifest, that two conjugial partners, are
the very forms and effigies of the marriage of love
and wisdom, or of good and truth.

> " Good and truth in God alone
> Shine with undivided ray ;
> Creatures that surround his throne,
> These through diff'rent forms display :
> Still the more those forms unite,
> Life has more of pure delight.
>
> " Thus the virtuous man may trace,
> In the softer female mind,
> Love with each attractive grace,
> Each affection more refin'd ;
> While *his* reason's steady course,
> Gives to sweetness all its force.
>
> " Woman thus on man relying,
> Finds out wisdom's bright abode ;
> Each another self descrying,
> Social comforts cheer the road :
> Harmony to life is given,
> Earth resumes the form of heaven."

SECTION IV.

SHEWING how that none can enter Heaven, so as to take up his eternal abode there, but only they who are principled in Conjugial Love, or in the Heavenly Marriage of good and truth

" And when the king came in to see the guests, he saw there a man which had not on a WEDDING GARMENT."* MATT. xxii. 11, 13.

FEW at this day know what genuine conjugial love is, and whence it originates, by reason that few are

---

* To wear a *wedding-garment*, according to the Scripture-phrase, is to be principled in genuine truth originating in genuine goodness; or, what is the same thing, to be principled in true faith, grounded in real charity: but not to have on a wedding-garment, is to be in the mere possession of faith without charity, in which case the faith also is not genuine, and cannot be endured in heaven, even should a hypocrite now and then, as appears, from the case of the man without a wedding-garment in the parable, to be not impossible, insinuate himself into that kingdom. All who honour the Lord as a Redeemer and Saviour only with the mouth and lips, whilst with the heart and spirit they look at Him as a mere man, are meant by him, who entered into the marriage *not having on a wedding-garment;* the wedding-garment is faith in the Lord as the Son of God—God of heaven and earth, and one with the Father.

principled in that love; it is almost universally believed to be innate, and thus to flow from a certain natural instinct, as it is called, and this the rather, because even amongst other animals there exists a conjugal principle; when yet the difference between conjugial love amongst mankind, and the conjugal principle which hath place amongst other animals, is like the difference between the state of man, and the state of a brute creature. And whereas few at this day, as was observed, know what conjugial love is, therefore from what hath been discovered respecting it, we shall describe it: Conjugial love deriveth its origin from the Divine Marriage of Good and Truth, consequently from the Lord Himself: that this is the origin of conjugial love, doth not appear to outward sense and apprehension, but still it may be manifest from influx, and from correspondence, and moreover from the Word; from INFLUX, inasmuch as heaven, by virtue of the union of good and of truth, which flows from the Lord, is compared to a marriage, and is called a marriage; from CORRESPONDENCE, inasmuch as when good united with truth flows down into an inferior sphere, it forms an union of minds, and when into a still lower sphere, it forms a marriage, wherefore an union of minds, by virtue of good united with truth from the Lord, is essential conjugial love. That this is the source of genuine conjugial love, may appear also from this consideration, that no one can be in it, unless he be principled in the good of truth and in the truth of good from the Lord; and likewise from this consideration, that heavenly blessedness and happiness is in that love, and they who are in it, all come into heaven, or into the heavenly marriage; hence it is, that in the WORD, the union of good and of truth is called a marriage, but the adulteration of good, and the falsification of truth, is called adultery and whoredom.

That to marry denotes to be conjoined to the Lord, and that to enter into the marriage denotes to be received into heaven by the Lord, is evident from the following passages: "The kingdom of heaven is like unto a certain king, who made a marriage for his son, and sent forth servants and invited to the marriage," &c. Matt. xxii. 1—14.: "The kingdom of heaven is like to ten virgins, who went forth to meet the Bridegroom, of whom five being prepared entered into the marriage," Matt. xxv. 1, and the following verses; that the Lord here meant Himself, is evident from verse 13, of the same chapter, where it is said, "Watch, because ye know not the day nor the hour, in which the Son of Man is about to come;" also from the Revelation, "The time of the marriage of the Lamb is come, and His Wife hath made herself ready: Blessed are they who are called to the marriage supper of the Lamb," chap. xix 7, 9. Marriages, therefore, are given in the heavens, as in the world, but to no others there, except to those who are in the marriage of good and truth, neither are others angels; wherefore spiritual marriages, which are those of good and truth, are not there

given; these are given in the world, and not after
man's decease, thus not in the heavens, as it is said
of the five foolish virgins, who were even invited to
the marriage, that they could not enter, because
they had not the marriage of good and truth, for
they had no oil but only lamps; by oil is meant
good, and by lamps truth; and to be given in marriage is to enter into heaven, where is the marriage
of good and truth. They who in a married state,
during the life of the body, have enjoyed the
happiness resulting from genuine conjugial love,
enjoy the same happiness also in another life; so that
the happiness of one life is continued to them
in that of another, and in the other life there
is effected an union of minds, in which is heaven. I
have been told, that the kinds of celestial and
spiritual happinesses thence derived, according to the
most general view only, are indefinite in number. I
have been informed, that genuine conjugial love
is essential innocence which dwells in wisdom;
they who have lived in conjugial love, are principled in wisdom above all others in heaven.
With those who live in conjugial love, the interior
principles of the mind are open through heaven
even to the Lord, for that love flows from the Lord
through man's inmost principle; hence they have
the kingdom of the Lord in themselves, and hence
they have genuine love towards infants for the sake
of the Lord's kingdom; and hence too they are receptible of heavenly loves more than other persons,
and are also more highly principled in mutual love,

for mutual love floweth thence as a stream from its fountain.

The ground and reason why the love of the sex remaineth with man after death, is, because after death a male is a male and a female a female, and the male principle in the male is male (or masculine) in the whole and in every part thereof; in like manner the female principle in the female, and a principle tending to conjunction, is in all and singular their parts, yea, in the most singular; and whereas this conjunctive principle was implanted from creation, and thence perpetually influences, it follows, that the one desires and breathes after conjunction with the other. Love considered in itself is nothing else but a desire and consequent tendency to conjunction, and conjugial love to conjunction into one; for the male man and the female man were so created, that from two they may become as one man, or one flesh, and when they become one, they are then, taken together, man in his fulness; but without such conjunction, they are two, and each is as a divided or half-man. Now, whereas the above conjunctive principle lies inmostly concealed in all and singular the parts of the male, and in all and singular the parts of the female, and the same is true of the faculty and desire to be conjoined together into one, it follows, that the mutual and reciprocal love of the sex remaineth with men (*homines*) after death.

Hence it may appear that in the heavens there

are marriages equally as in the world, but in the
heavens marriages are made of like with like, for
the man is born to act from understanding, but the
woman from affection, and understanding with men,
is the understanding of truth and good, and affection
with women is the affection of truth and good; and
whereas all understanding derives life from affection, therefore they are coupled together, as the
affection which is of the will is coupled with correspondent thought, which is of the understanding;
for understanding with every one is various, as the
truths are various from which it is formed; in ge-
eral there are celestial truths, there are spiritual
truths, there are moral truths, there are civil truths,
yea, there are natural truths, and of every truth there
are innumerable species and varieties; and whereas
it hence comes to pass that the understanding of one
person is in no case like that another, nor the affection of one like the affection of another, therefore
to the intent that understanding and affection,
may nevertheless act in unity, they are so coupled
together in heaven, that the correspondent affection,
which is of the woman, is joined with a correspondent understanding, which is of the man; hence it
is that each hath life from the correspondence full
of love.

Inasmuch now as two various affections cannot
correspond to one understanding, hence in heaven
it is in no case given, nor can be given, that one
man shall have more wives than one; from these

considerations it may be seen and concluded, what is also spiritually meant by a *man leaving father and mother and cleaving to his wife, and becoming one flesh*, viz. that a man shall leave what is evil and false, which appertains to him in a religious view, and which defiles his understanding; thus which he hath from father and mother, and that his understanding, separated from them, shall be conjoined with a correspondent affection, which is of the wife, whence two become one affection of truth and of good ; this is meant by the *one flesh*, in which the two shall be, for *flesh*, in the spiritual sense, signifies the good which is of love or affection : and that the words *wherefore they are no longer two, but one flesh*, signify that thus the understanding of good and truth, and the affection of good and truth, *are not two, but one*, in like manner as will and understanding indeed are two, but still one; in like manner also as truth and good ; likewise faith and charity, which indeed are two, but still one, viz. when truth is of good and good is of truth, also when faith is of charity, and charity of faith; hence likewise conjugial love is derived. The reason why Moses, *on account of hardness of heart, permitted to put away a wife for every cause,* was because the Israelites and Jews were natural, and not spiritual, and they who are merely natural are hard of heart, because they are not in any conjugial love, but in lascivious love, such as is that of adultery; hence also they are called "An evil and adulterous generation," Matt. xii. 39. " A wicked and adulterous generation," chap. xvi. 4. The reason why *whosoever shall put away a wife, except for fornication, and shall marry another, committeth adultery,* is, because fornication signifieth what is false, and with the woman the affection of what is evil and false, thus an affection which in no sort agrees with the understanding of truth and good, and hence heaven and the church altogether perish with man, for when interior conjunction, which is that of minds, is annulled, marriage is dissolved : The reason why he that *marrieth her who is put away, also committeth adultery,* is, because by her that is put away on account of fornication, is meant the affection of what is evil and false, as above, which is not to be coupled with any understanding of truth and good, for hence the understanding is perverted, and also becomes an understanding of what is false and evil, and the conjunction of what is false and evil is spiritual adultery, as the conjunction of what is true and good is spiritual marriage.   Now as adulteries are contrary to conjugial love, it is not possible for adulterers to be with the angels in heaven ; their contrariety also to goodness and truth is a cause of separation ; for the same reason it is impossible they should be in the heavenly marriage, which is rendered further impossible by the filthy ideas they entertain concerning marriage ; when marriage is only mentioned, and an idea thereof occurs, instantly their ideas are filled with lascivious, obscene, and wicked abominations ; in like manner, when the angels discourse concerning goodness and truth, adulterers think contrary thereto; for all affections, and thoughts thence derived, remain with man after death, such as they have been in the world. Thus in their hearts being contrary to charity and mercy, adulterers are generally cruel, making mock at the miseries of others, desiring to deprive others of their property, and practising such desires as far as they dare, delighting in the destruction of friendships, and in sowing the seeds of enmities; they pretend to a religious principle, in that they say they acknowledge the Creator of the universe, and a Providence but only universal, and salvation grounded in faith, and that their lot will not be worse than that of others; but when they are explored as to their qualities in heart, which is done in another life, it is then discovered that they do not even believe these things, but instead of the Creator of the universe, they acknowledge nature; instead of an universal Providence, they acknowledge no Providence, and respecting faith they think nothing; and all this as a consequence of the utter opposition of adulteries to goodness and truth; hence every one may judge how adulterers can come into heaven.

But it is a certain fact, that the conjugial principle, which is the very ground-work of regeneration, is capable of being ingrafted in christians, and of being transplanted hereditarily into the offspring, from parents who are principled in love

truly conjugial, and that hence both the faculty and
inclination to grow wise in the things of the church
and of heaven, may become connate. That children
derive from their parents inclinations to such things
as had been objects of love and of life with the parents, is a truth most perfectly agreeable to the testimony of history in general, and of experience in
particular; but that they do not derive or inherit
from their parents the affections themselves, and
thence the lives of those affections, but only inclinations, and also faculties thereto. That children, to the latest posterity, by virtue of innate
inclinations, if they are not broken, are led into affections, thoughts, speech, and life, similar to those
of their parents, is clearly manifest from the Jewish nation, in that at this day they are like unto
their fathers in Egypt, in the wilderness, in the
land of Canaan, and in the Lord's time; and that
this likeness is not confined to their minds only, but
extends to their countenances; for who doth not
know a Jew by his look? The case is the same with
the descendants of others. From these considerations
it may infallibly be concluded, that children are
born with inclinations to such things as their parents were inclined to.   But it is of the Divine
Providence, that thought and act should not follow
inclination, to the intent that perverse inclinations
may be rectified : it is also of the Divine Providence
that a faculty hath been implanted for this purpose,
by virtue whereof, parents and masters have the
power of amending the morals of children, and chil-

dren may afterwards amend their own morals, when they come to years of discretion.

The reason why children born of parents who are principled in love truly conjugial, derive inclinations and faculties—if a son, to perceive the things appertaining to wisdom, and if a daughter, to love the things which wisdom teaches—is, because the conjugial principle of good and truth is implanted from creation in every soul, and also in the principles derived from the soul; for that principle flows into man from the Lord, and constitutes his human life: it also filleth the universe from first principles to last, and from a man even to a worm; and that along with it, the faculty to open the inferior principles of the mind, even to conjunction with its superior principles, which are in the light and heat of heaven, is also implanted in every man from creation; hence it is evident, that a superior suitableness and facility to conjoin good to truth, and truth to good, and thus to grow wise, is inherited by those who are born from such marriage; consequently they have a superior suitableness and facility also to imbibe the things appertaining to the church and heaven; for conjugial love is conjoined with these things, and this because love truly conjugial keeps pace with the state of the church in man.

I have been informed by the angels, that they who lived in the most ancient times, live at this day in the heavens, houses and houses, families and families, nations and nations, in like manner as they had lived on earth, and that scarce any one of a house is wanting; and that the reason is, because they were principled in love truly conjugial; and that hence their children inherited inclinations to the conjugial principle of good and truth, and that they were easily initiated into it, more and more interiorly, by education received from their parents; and afterwards, as from themselves, when they became capable of judging for themselves, were introduced into it by the Lord.* From these considerations, reason may discover the end for which the Lord the Creator hath provided, and still provides, marriages of love truly conjugal.

---

* It is undoubtedly in consequence of the vast accumulation of hereditary evil, which has been going on increasing, and handing down from father to son, without interruption, for a long succession of ages, that conjugial love, or regeneration, is both so very rare and difficult of attainment at the present day. Whereas, were children to be born of parents who had previously become regenerate, there is reason to believe that hereditary evil would gradually be diminished, till at length the whole human race, or at least the men of the church, would again come into the same blessed state in which they lived in the most ancient times, and in which our first parents, or rather the first church, signified by Adam and Eve, originally stood.

SECTION V.

SHEWING how all who have been spiritually married or regenerated in the world, or who have died in a state of preparation for it, will each be united in Heaven to his true conjugial partner.

"And they that WERE READY went in with Him to the marriage." MATT. xxv. 10.

THERE are two states into which a man enters after death, an external and an internal state; he comes first into his external state, and afterwards into his internal; and during the external state, married partners meet each other, (supposing they are both deceased,) know each other, and if they have lived together in the world, associate again, and for some time live together;* and when they are in this state, they do not know the inclination of each to the other, this being concealed in the

---

* It is taught in the New Church, as well as in the Church of Rome, though viewed in a very different light, that there is an intermediate place or state of existence between heaven and hell, into which the spirit enters immediately on its separation from the body at death, and which is called the *world of spirits,* to

internals of each : but afterwards, when they come into their internal state, the inclination manifests itself, and if it be in mutual agreement and sympathy, they continue to live together a conjugial life, but if it be in disagreement and antipathy, their marriage is dissolved. In case the man had had

distinguish it from the *spiritual world,* which comprehends the spiritual state of existence in general, including both the intermediate state, and heaven and hell. It is in the *world of spirits,* therefore, that married partners meet after death, and there it is that the real state of their hearts and affections towards each other is known, when they either again unite and live together as husband and wife, or, if their minds be not in agreement, are finally separated.

The end or design of this intermediate state, according to our Author is, not that any one can either be made better or worse there, as to his real and internal character, agreeable to the saying,—" *where the tree falleth, so it lieth;*" but that the man who is not as yet fully prepared for his eternal abode, either in heaven or hell, may undergo such a state of vastation, as that his external may be like his internal, or, in other words, that he may not be of a double mind: Thus, for instance, if a man be in possession of certain truths which he had become acquainted with in the body, and in which he professed a belief, but yet led a life at variance with them ; he is there dispossessed of those truths, and left only to think and believe what is in agreement with his life's love, which of course can only be what is false and erroneous, though to him it may appear otherwise : while on the other hand, with the man who had led a good and useful life in the world, according to the light he enjoyed, but who notwithstanding, was in many mistaken notions, he is there better instructed, and initiated into more correct ideas of divine things; agreeably to what is written,—" For *whosoever*

several wives, he successively joins himself with them, whilst he is in his external state; but when he enters into his internal state, in which he perceives the inclination of love, and of what quality they are, he then either adopts one, or leaves all; for in the spiritual world, as well as in the natural world, it is not allowable for any christian to have more than one wife, inasmuch as it infests and profanes religion. The case is the same with the woman who had had several husbands; nevertheless the women in this case do not join themselves to their

---

hath, to him shall be given, and he shall have more abundance; but whosoever hath not, from him shall be taken away even that he hath," Matt. xiii. 12.; xxv. 29. Mark iv. 25. Luke viii. 18.

That there is such an intermediate state of existence, is not in general believed amongst Protestants, in consequence of its being discarded as an erroneous doctrine, at least as professed in the Romish church; notwithstanding, however, it is confirmed by a variety of passages in the Sacred Scriptures. Without taking up room here to discuss the subject, it may be sufficient to mention, that it was in this intermediate state in which St John the Revelator saw his visions, as well as the other prophets in the Old Testament; for in the state in which he then was, he repeatedly speaks of heaven being above and hell beneath, as well as of things there similar to what are here, such as earth, sea, trees, animals, &c but all, of course, of a spiritual nature and origin. Some again have actually been let into heaven, or at least permitted to see into it, as St John himself was, and likewise the Apostle Paul. But for further confirmation, on this interesting point, the Reader is referred to the work, ON HEAVEN AND HELL

husbands, they only present themselves, and the husbands adjoin them to themselves. It is to be noted, that husbands rarely know their wives, but that wives well know their husbands; the reason is, because women have an interior perception of love, and men only an exterior.

The reason why separations take place after death, is, because the conjunctions which are made on earth are seldom made from any internal perception of love, but from an external perception which hides the internal; the external perception of love originates in such things as regard the love of the world and of the body; wealth and large possessions are peculiarly the objects of worldly love, whilst dignities and honours are those of the love of the body; besides these objects, there are also various enticing allurements, such as beauty and an external polish of manners, and sometimes even an unchasteness of character, which lead to external conjunctions; moreover, matrimonial engagements are frequently contracted within the particular district, city, or village, in which the parties were born, and where they inhabit, in which case the choice is confined and limited to families which are known, and to such as are in similar circumstances in life; hence it is, that matrimonial connections made in the world are for the most part external, and not at the same time internal; when yet it is the internal conjunction, or conjunction of souls, which constitutes a real marriage, and this conjunction is not perceivable, until man puts off the external and puts on the internal, as is the case after death. This then is the ground and reason why separations take place, and afterwards new conjunctions with such as are similar and homogeneous, unless these conjunctions have been provided on earth, as is the case with those who, from an early age, have loved, have wished, and have asked of the Lord a legitimate and lovely connection with one of the sex, shunning and abominating the impulses of a loose and wandering lust.

In what manner marriages are contracted in the heavens, it hath also been granted me to see: in heaven throughout, there is a consociation of those who are of similar dispositions, and a dissociation of those who are of dissimilar; hence every society of heaven consists of those who are of similar dispositions; similar are presented to similar, not of themselves, but from the Lord; in like manner one conjugial partner is presented to another conjugial partner, where there is a capacity of their minds being conjoined into one; wherefore at first sight they intimately love each other, and see themselves to be conjugial partners, and enter into marriage; hence it is, that all the marriages of heaven are from the Lord alone: they also have their festivities, which take place in the company of several; the festivities differ in different societies. It is for this reason that marriages in the heavens are contracted with those who are within a society, because they are in similar good and truth, but not with those who are out of the society: this was also represented in the Israelitish nation by marriages being contracted within tribes, and specifically within families and not out of them.

With those who are regenerated, there is given after death to the man a suitable wife, and to the woman a suitable husband; the reason is, because no other married partners can be received into heaven, so as to remain there, but such as have been interiorly united, or are capable of being united as in one, for in heaven two married partners are not called two, but one angel; which is understood by the Lord's words, that they are no longer two, but one flesh. The reason why no other married partners are received into heaven, is, because no others can there cohabit, that is, abide together in one house, and in one bed-chamber and bed; for all who are in the heavens, are associated together according to affinities and relationships of love, and have habitations accordingly, inasmuch as in the spiritual world there are not spaces, but appearances of spaces, and these appearances are according to the states of life of the inhabitants, and the states of life are according to the states of love; wherefore in that world no one can dwell but in one house, which is provided for and assigned to him according to the quality of his love; if he dwells in any other, he is straitened and pained in his breast and breathing; and it is impossible for two to cohabit in the

same house, unless they are likenesses; neither anc
married partners so cohabit, unless they are mutual
inclinations; if they are external inclinations, and
not internal at the same time, the very house itself,
or the place itself, separates, rejects, and drives
them away. This is the reason why, for those, who
after preparation are introduced into heaven, there
is provided marriage with a consort whose soul in-
clines to mutual union with the soul of another, so
that they no longer wish to be two lives, but one:
and this is the reason also, why after separation
there is given to the man a suitable wife, and to
the woman in like manner a suitable husband.

That after death a suitable wife is given to a husband, and a suitable husband to a wife, and that
they enjoy delightful and ,blessed communications,
but without prolification, except of a spiritual kind,
is to be understood of those who are received into
heaven, and become angels; the reason is, because
such are spiritual, and marriages in themselves are
spiritual, and thence holy: but with respect to those
who go to hell, they are all natural; and marriages
merely natural are not marriages, but conjunctions
which originate in unchaste lust.

The ground and reason why conjugial pairs enjoy
similar communications as in the world, is, because
after death a male is a male, and a female a female,
and there is implanted in each at creation, an inclination to conjunction; and this inclination with
man is the inclination of his spirit and thence of

D

his body; wherefore after death, when man becomes a spirit, the same mutual inclination remains, and this cannot exist without similar communications; for after death man is man as before, neither is any thing wanting in the male, nor any thing in the female; as to form they are like themselves, and also as to affections and thoughts; and what must be the necessary consequence, but that they must enjoy like communications? And whereas conjugial love is chaste, pure, and holy, therefore their communications are in all fulness and blessedness. The reason why such communications are more delightful and blessed than in the world, is, because conjugial love, when it is the love of a spirit, becomes more interior and pure, and thereby more perceivable, and every delight increases according to perception, and increases to such a degree, that its blessedness is distinguishable in its delight. The reason also why marriages in the heavens are without prolification, and that in place thereof there is experienced spiritual prolification, which is that of love and wisdom, is, because with the inhabitants of the spiritual world, the third or ultimate principle, which is natural, is wanting, and this principle is the continent of spiritual principles, and spiritual principles without their continent have no consistence, like those principles which are procreated in the natural world; moreover, spiritual principles considered in themselves have relation to love and wisdom, wherefore love and wisdom are the births produced from marriages in the heavens : these are called births, because conjugial love perfects an angel, uniting him with his consort, in consequence whereof both together become more and more a man *(homo)*, for, as was said above, two conjugial partners in heaven are not two but one angel; wherefore by conjugial unition they fill themselves with the human principle, which consists in desiring to grow wise, and in loving whatsoever appertains to wisdom.

They who are in love truly conjugial, after death, when they become angels, return into youth and adolescence; the males, however worn out with age, become young men; and the wives, however worn out with age, become young women ; each conjugial partner returns into the flower and into the joys of the age in which love conjugial beginneth to exalt the life with new delights, and to inspire sportiveness for the sake of prolification : into this state, first exteriorly, afterwards more and more interiorly to eternity, cometh the man who had fled adulteries as sins, and was inaugurated by the Lord into conjugial love, whilst he lived in the world. Inasmuch as they are always growing young more interiorly, it follows that love truly conjugial increaseth, and entereth into its delights and satisfactions, which were provided for it from the creation of the world, and which are the delights and satisfactions of the inmost heaven arising from the love of the Lord towards heaven and the church, and thence from the

love of good and truth towards each other, from
which loves is derived every joy in the heavens.
The reason why man thus groweth young in heaven,
is, because he then entereth into the marriage of good
and truth, and there is in good an effort of continually
loving truth, and in truth there is an effort of continually loving good, and then the wife is good in
its form, and the man is truth in its form: from
that effort man putteth off all the severity, sadness,
and dryness appertaining to age, and puts on the
liveliness, gladness, and freshness of youth, from
which the effort liveth and becometh joy. It hath
been told me from heaven, that they have then a life
of love, which cannot otherwise be described, than
as being the life of joy itself. From conjugial love
the angels derive all their beauty; thus each angel is
beautiful according to that love: for all the angels
are forms of their own affections, inasmuch as in
heaven it is not allowed to feign with the face, things
which are not of the affection; wherefore the face of
the angels is a type of their mind; whilst therefore
they have conjugial love, they have love to the Lord,
mutual love, the love of good and the love of truth,
and the love of wisdom: these loves with them form
their faces, and present themselves as fires of life in
their eyes, to which moreover innocence and peace
are added, which complete their beauty. Such
forms are the forms of the inmost angelic heaven,
and are forms truly human.

   That love truly conjugial, containeth in itself so

many ineffable delights as to exceed all number and expression, may also appear from this consideration, that that love is the fundamental of all loves celestial and spiritual, inasmuch as by it man becometh love, for from it one conjugial partner loveth another, as good loveth truth and truth loveth good, thus representatively as the Lord loveth heaven and the church: such love cannot exist otherwise than by marriage, in which the man is truth, and the wife is good. When man is made such love by marriage, then also he is in love to the Lord, and love towards his neighbour, consequently in the love of all good and in the love of all truth; for from man, as love, there cannot proceed any thing but loves of every kind: hence it is, that love conjugial is the fundamental love of all the loves of heaven: and inasmuch as it is the fundamental love of all the loves of heaven, it is also the fundamental of all the delights and joys of heaven, for every delight and joy is of love: from these considerations it follows, that heavenly joys, in their order and in their degrees, derive their origins and causes from conjugial love.

From the felicities of marriage a conclusion may be drawn respecting the infelicities of adulteries, namely, that the love of adultery is the fundamental of all infernal loves, which in themselves are not loves, but hatreds: consequently, that it is the love of adultery from which flow hatreds of every kind, as well against God as against the neighbour, in

general against all the good and truth of heaven and
the church, whence to it belong all infelicities; for
as was before said, from adulteries man becometh a
form of hell, and from the love thereof an image of
the devil. That from marriages, in which is love
truly conjugial, all delights and felicities increase
even to the delights and felicities of the inmost heaven; and that all that is undelightful and unhappy
in marriages, in which the love of adultery reigns,
increases in direfulness even to the lowest hell, may
be seen in the work concerning HEAVEN AND HELL,
n. 386.

All delights whatsoever, of which man. hath any
sensation, are delights of his love, the love mani-
festing itself, yea, existing and living thereby; that
delights are exalted in the same degree that the love
is exalted, and also in the same degree that the in-
cident affections touch the ruling love more nearly,
is a known thing. Now, whereas conjugial love is
the foundation love of all good loves, and whereas it is inscribed on all parts and principles of
man, even the most particular, it follows that the
delights thereof, exceed the delights of all other
loves, and also that it gives delight to the other
loves, according to its presence and conjunction
with them; for it expands the inmost principles of
the mind, and at the same time the inmost principles of the body, as the delightful current of its
fountain flows through and opens. The reason why
all delights from first to last are collated into this

love, is on account of the superior excellence of its use, which is the propagation of the human race, and thence of the angelic heaven; and whereas this use was the end of all ends of creation, it follows that all the blessednesses, satisfactions, delights, pleasantnesses, and pleasures, which the Lord the Creator could possibly collate into man, are collated into this love. That delights follow use, and are also communicated to man according to the love thereof, is manifest from the delights of the five senses, seeing, hearing, smelling, taste, and touch; each of these has its delights, with variations according to the specific uses of each; what then must be the delight annexed to the sense of conjugial love, the use of which is the complex of all other uses? Moreover the angels have related wonderful things respecting these delights, adding further, that their varieties in the souls of conjugial pairs, and from their souls in their minds, and from their minds in their breasts, are infinite and eternal; and that they are exalted according to the prevalence of wisdom with the husband; and this because they live to eternity in the flower of their age, and because they know no greater blessedness than to grow wiser and wiser.*

But it is well to be observed, that no others come, nor can come into this love, that is, conjugial love,

* See note at page 14, for the Author's meaning, as to the term *to grow wise.*

except such as come to the Lord, and love the truths
of the church, and practise its goods. The ground
and reason why no others can be principled in love
truly conjugial, but they who receive it from the
Lord, is because this love, considered in its origin and its correspondence, is celestial, spiritual,
holy, pure, and clean, above every love implanted in the angels of heaven and the men of the
church; and these its distinguishing characters and
qualities cannot possibly be given, and have existence, except with those who are joined to the Lord,
and by virtue of such conjunction are consociated
with the angels of heaven; for these shun extra-
conjugial loves, which are conjunctions with others
than their own proper conjugial partner, as they
would shun the loss of the soul and the lakes of
hell; and in proportion as conjugial partners shun
such conjunctions, even as to the libidinous desires
of the will, and the intentions thence derived, so far
love truly conjugial is purified with them, and becometh successively spiritual, first during their
abode on earth, and afterwards in heaven. It is
not, however, possible that any love should become
perfectly pure with men, nor with angels, consequently neither this love; nevertheless, since the
intention of the will is what the Lord principally
regards, therefore, so far as man is in this intention,
and perseveres in it, so far he is initiated into its
purity and sanctity, and successively advances
therein.

That there is given such a conjugial love as is described above, may indeed be acknowledged from the first state of that love, when it insinuates itself and enters into the hearts of a youth and a virgin; thus from its influence on those who begin to love one of the sex, and to desire to be joined therewith in marriage; and still more at the time of courtship and the interval which precedes the marriage ceremony; and lastly, during the marriage ceremony and some days after it; at such times, who doth not acknowledge and consent to the following positions, that this love is the foundation love of all loves, and also that into it are collated all joys and all delights from first to last? And who doth not know, that, after this season of pleasure, the satisfactions thereof successively pass away and are gone, till at length they are scarce sensible? In this latter case, if it be said as before, that this love is the foundation love of all loves, and that into it are collated all joys and delights, the positions are not agreed to nor acknowledged, and possibly it will be asserted that they are nonsense, or incomprehensible mysteries. From these considerations it is evident, that primitive marriage love bears a resemblance to love truly conjugial, and exhibits it visible in a certain image; the reason whereof is, because in such a case, the promiscuous love of the sex is cast away, which is unchaste love, and in its place the love of one of the sex, which is love truly conjugial and chaste, remains implanted: in this case, who doth not regard other women with a look of indifference, and the one to whom he is united, with a look of love and affection?

The reason why love truly conjugial is notwithstanding so rare, that its quality is not known, and scarce its existence, is, because the state of pleasurable gratifications before and at the time of marriage, is afterwards changed into a state of indifference arising from an insensibility to such gratifications; the causes of this change of state are too numerous to be here adduced; indeed, with the generality at this day, this image of conjugial love is so abolished, and with the image the knowledge thereof, that its quality, and even its existence, are scarce known. It is a known thing, however, that every man is by birth merely corporeal, and that from corporeal he becomes natural more and more interiorly, and thus rational, and at length spiritual; the reason why this is effected progressively, is, because the corporeal principle is like ground, wherein things natural, rational, and spiritual, are implanted in their order; thus man becomes more and more man. The case is nearly similar when he enters into marriage; on this occasion man becomes a fuller man, because he is joined with a consort, with whom he acts as one man; but this, in the first state spoken of above, is effected only in a sort of image; in like manner, on this occasion he commences from what is corporeal, and proceeds to what is natural as to conjugial life, and thereby conjunction into one; they who, in this case, love corporeal natural things, and rational things only as grounded therein, cannot be conjoined to a consort as into one, except as to those external principles, and when those external principles fail, cold invades the internal principles, in consequence whereof the delights of that love are dispersed and driven away, as from the mind so from the body, and afterwards as from the body so from the mind, and this until there is nothing left remaining of the remembrance of the primæval state of their marriage, consequently nothing of knowledge respecting it. Now, whereas this is the case with the generality of persons at this day, it is evident that love truly conjugial is not known as to its quality, and scarce as to its existence. It is otherwise with those who are spiritual; the first state with such is an initiation into perpetual satisfactions, which advance in degree, so far as the spiritual rational principle of the mind, and thence the natural sensual principle of the body, in each party, conjoin and unite themselves with the same principles in the other party; but such instances are rare.

To what hath been above related concerning the state of conjugial partners after death, it may be expedient to add the following circumstances. I. That all those married partners, who are merely natural, are separated after death; the reason is, because the love of marriage grows cold with such, and the love of adultery grows warm. II. Married partners, of which one is spiritual and the ether natural, are also separated after death, and to the spiritual is given a suitable conjugial partner, whereas the natural one is transmitted to the resorts of the lascivious amongst his like in hell. III. But they who in the world have lived a single life, and have altogether alienated their minds from marriage, in case they be spiritual, remain single, but if natural, they become whoremongers. It is otherwise with those, who, in their single state, have desired marriage, and especially if they have solicited it without success; for such, in case they are spiritual, blessed marriages are provided, but not until they come into heaven. IV. They who in the world have been shut up in monasteries, both men and women, at the conclusion of the monastic life, which continues some time after death, are let loose, and discharged, and enjoy the free indulgence of their desires, whether they are disposed to live in a married state, or not; if they are disposed to live in a married state, this is granted them, but if otherwise, they are conveyed to those who live in celibacy on the side of heaven; such, however, as have indulged the fires of prohibited lust are cast down. V. The reason why they who live in celibacy are on the side of heaven, is because the sphere of perpetual celibacy infests the sphere of conjugial love, which is the very essential sphere of heaven; and the reason why the sphere of conjugial love is the very essential sphere of heaven, is, because it descends from the heavenly marriage of the Lord and the church.

SECTION VI.

*SHEWING how marriages in heaven are to be reconcil-
ed with the LORD'S words, where He saith, that,
after the resurrection, they neither marry
nor are given in marriage.*

"Wherefore they are no more twain, but one flesh. What therefore God hath joined together, let not man put asunder." MATT.
xix. 6.

INASMUCH as heaven is from the human race, and hence the angels therein are of both sexes; and whereas it is ordained from creation that the woman should be for the man, and the man for the woman, thus each should be the other's; and since that love is innate in each, it follows that there are marriages in the heavens as well as on the earth: but marriages in the heavens differ greatly from marriages on the earth. What, therefore, is the nature and quality of marriages in the heavens, and in what they differ from marriages on the earth, and in what they agree, shall now be shewn in what follows.

E

That there are marriages in heaven cannot be admitted as an article of faith with those, who imagine that man after death is a soul or spirit, and whose idea of a soul or spirit, is as of an attenuated æther or vapour; who imagine also, that man will not live as man till after the day of the last judgment, and, in general, who know nothing respecting the spiritual world, in which dwell angels and spirits, consequently in which are heavens and hells: and whereas that world hath been heretofore unknown, and mankind been in total ignorance that the angels of heaven are men in a perfect form, and in like manner infernal spirits, but in an imperfect form; therefore it was not possible for any thing to be revealed concerning marriages in that world; for it would in such case have been objected, How can soul be joined with soul, or vapour with vapour, as one married partner with another here on earth? Not to mention many more like objections, which, the instant they were made, would take away and dissipate all faith respecting marriages in another life: but now inasmuch as several particulars have been revealed concerning that world, and a description hath been also given of its nature and quality, as hath been done in the treatise on HEAVEN AND HELL, and also in the APOCALYPSE REVEALED, it is possible that the assertion respecting marriages, as having place in that world, may be established and confirmed, even so as to convince the reason.

That man liveth a man after death, hath been heretofore unknown in the world, for the reasons just now mentioned : and what is surprising, it hath been unknown even in the christian world, where the Word is, and thence illustration concerning life eternal, and where the Lord Himself teacheth, *that all the dead rise again, and that God is not the God of the dead, but of the living,* Matt. xxii. 31, 32. Luke xx. 37, 38. Moreover, man as to the affections and thoughts of his mind, is in the midst of angels and spirits, and is so consociated with them that he cannot be plucked asunder from them, but he instantly dies. It is still more surprising, that this is unknown, when yet every man who hath departed this life since the beginning of creation, after his decease, hath come, and doth still come, to his own ; or, as it is said in the Word, hath been gathered and is gathered to his own; besides, man hath a common (or general) perception, which is the same with the influx of heaven into the interiors of his mind, by virtue whereof he inwardly in himself perceiveth truths, and as it were seeth them, and especially this truth, that he liveth a man after death,—a happy man if he hath lived well, and unhappy if he hath lived ill : for who doth not think thus, whilst he elevates his mind in any degree above the body, and above the thought which borders next upon the senses, as is the case when he is engaged in divine worship from an interior principle, and when he lieth on his death bed, expecting his dissolution; in like manner when he hears of those who are deceased, and of their lot. I have related a thousand particulars respecting departed spirits, informing certain persons who are now alive, concerning the state of their deceased brethren, their married partners and friends. I have written also concerning the state of the English, the Dutch, the Papists, and Jews, the Gentiles, and likewise concerning the lot of Luther, of Calvin, and of Melancthon; and hitherto I never heard any one object, How can such be their lot, when as yet they are not risen from their sepulchres, the last judgment not being yet accomplished? Are not they in the meantime mere vapours and unsubstantial souls, residing in some place of confinement *(in quodam pu seu ubi)?* Such objections I have never as yet heard from any quarter, whence I have been led to conclude that every one perceives in himself that he liveth a man after death. Who, that hath loved his married partner, his infants and offspring, when they are dying, or are dead, will not say within himself (in case his thought be elevated above the sensual principles of the body) that they are in the hand of God, and that he shall see them again after his own death, and again be joined with them in a life of love and joy.

That man liveth a man after death, and that in this case a male is a male, and a female a female; and that every one's proper love remaineth with him after death, and that especially the love of the

sex, and conjugial love, remaineth, are positions
which I have wished hitherto to confirm by such
arguments as respect the understanding, and are
called rational: but whereas man, from his infancy,
in consequence of what hath been taught him by
his parents and masters, and afterwards by the
learned and the clergy, hath been induced to believe,
that he shall not live a man after death until the
day of the last judgment, which day hath now been
expected for six thousand years; and whereas several have regarded this article of faith as one of those
tenets, which ought to be believed, but not intellec-
tually conceived, it was therefore necessary that the
above positions should be confirmed also by ocular evidence; otherwise man, who believes only the senses,
in consequence of the faith previously implanted,
would object thus: If men lived as men after death,
I should certainly see and hear them: who hath
ever descended from heaven, or ascended out of hell,
to give such information? In reply to such objections, it is to be observed, that it never was possible, nor can be, that any angel of heaven should descend, or any spirit of hell ascend, and speak with
men, except with those who have the interiors of the
mind or spirit opened by the Lord; and this opening of the interiors cannot be fully effected, except
with those who have been prepared of the Lord to
receive the things which are of spiritual wisdom;
on which account it hath pleased the Lord to pre-
pare me, and to open the interiors of my mind, to
the intent that the state of heaven and hell, and the

state of the life of men after death, might not remain unknown, and be laid asleep in ignorance, and at length be buried in denial.

In respect to the Lord's words above referred to, on the subject of Marrriage, we shall quote the passage in the Evangelists at length :—"Certain of the Sadducees, who say that there is no resurrection, asked Jesus, saying, Master, Moses wrote, if a man die, having no children, his brother shall take his wife, and raise up seed unto his brother. Now there were with us seven brethren, and the first, when he had married a wife, deceased, and having no issue, left his wife unto his brother; likewise the second also, and the third, unto the seventh; last of all the woman died also: therefore, in the resurrection, whose wife shall she be of the seven? But Jesus answering, said unto them, The sons of this age marry and are given in marriage, but they who shall be accounted worthy to attain another age, and resurrection from the dead, shall neither marry nor be given in marriage, neither can they die any more, for they are like unto the angels, and are the sons of God, being sons of the resurrection. But that the dead rise again, even Moses shewed at the bush, when he calleth the Lord, the God of Abraham, and the God of Isaac, and the God of Jacob; for He is not the God of the dead, but of the living; for all live unto Him," Luke xx. 27—38. Matt. xxii. 22—31. There are two things which the Lord taught on this occasion, first, that man rises again after death; and secondly, that in heaven they are not given in marriage, or regenerated. That man rises again after death, He taught by these words, that God is not the God of the dead but of the living, and that Abraham, Isaac, and Jacob are alive; and further, in the parable concerning the rich man in hell, and Lazarus in heaven, Luke xvi. 22—31. Secondly, that in heaven they are not given in marriage, He taught by these words, that *they who are accounted worthy to attain the other age, neither marry nor are given in marriage.* That no other marriages are here meant, than spiritual or interior marriages, is manifest from the words which immediately follow, that they can no longer die, because they are like to the angels and the sons of God, being sons of the resurrection. By spiritual marriage is meant conjunction with the Lord, thus regeneration; and this is effected on earth, and when it is effected on earth, it is effected also in the heavens; wherefore in the heavens such marriage is not again repeated, nor are they given in marriage. This also is meant by these words, *the sons of this age marry and are given in marriage, but they who are accounted worthy to attain the other age, neither marry nor are given in marriage:* These also are by the Lord called *sons of the marriage,* Matt. ix. 15. Mark ii. 19., and now *angels, sons of God,* and *sons of the resurrection,* which evidently mean the regenerate.

"Whether, therefore, we speak of marriage, or of conjunction with the Lord, it is the same thing; and whether we speak of love truly conjugial, or of that conjunction, it is still the same thing. But conjunction with the Lord of Heaven, it is allowed in the church, can only be effected by *repentance* and *regeneration ;* and of course, without repentance and regeneration, there can be no true marriage, or true conjugial love; and whether we talk of repenting and of being regenerated, or of marrying and being given in a marriage, it is the same thing. Let it be supposed now, that instead of saying, "In the resurrection they neither marry, nor are given in marriage," the Lord had said, " In the resurrection they neither *repent,* nor are *made regenerate,* (repentance and regeneration being works which cannot be wrought in the other life,) who would have thought it a just or reasonable conclusion from such words, to urge, that after death, the penitent and regenerate, did not live in a penitent and regenerate state? Yet, as little of justice and of reason is there in the conclusion, that after death, truly married partners do not live in a married state, because the Lord hath said, that *in the resurrection they neither marry nor are given in marriage.* In short, there is a wide difference between asserting, that in the resurrection they neither marry nor are given in marriage; and asserting, that in the resurrection married partners, who are united by love truly conjugial, do not live together in a married state. The former assertion is an important and eternal truth, declaring, that *hereafter* there can be no conjunction formed with the Lord of Heaven, unless it hath in some measure been wrought in this life; whereas the latter assertion is, to insist that conjunction with the Lord, and consequent conjunction of minds and bodies, ceases hereafter, which is the same thing as saying, that heaven itself ceases : for what heaven can remain, if there be no conjunction with the Lord? And who can suppose it probable, or possible, that the minds of married partners should be conjoined with the Lord in this world, and not be conjoined with Him in a future life; or that they should be conjoined with each other in the Lord here, and not be conjoined with each other in the Lord hereafter? It is plain then, that the above words of the Lord prove nothing, and were not intended to prove any thing, against married partners living hereafter in the enjoyments of love truly conjugial, but only against the possibility of any one entering into those enjoyments after death, who hath not attained to some degree of initiation into the preparatory love during his abode in this world."*

" Who, for instance, that has been tenderly and virtuously attached to a female, and has walked with her in the path to heaven, would not feel it a grievous blow to his happiness, should he find her, there, totally unlike the being he knew here? Could there even be any perfect social happiness in a so-

---

* See *Preface to the Treatise* On Conjugial and Scortatory Love.

ciety consisting of all males, or all neuters? Independently of its use in the continuance of the species, is not the division into sexes a most beneficent arrangement, immensely adding to the comforts, and harmonizing the intercourses, of the human race? Is it not then reasonable to conclude, that this use of it will be perpetuated, where the former ceases? And is it not the essence of reason to conclude, that a union in which, in its genuine state, is concentered all that is heavenly on earth,—including a love which prefers another's welfare to its own, and a joy which nothing but such a love can inspire,—must, when exalted to its highest perfection, be among the highest beatitudes of heaven itself?

> " Whatever hypocrites austerely talk
> Of purity, and place, and innocence,
> Defaming as impure what God declares
> Pure,   *   *   *   *
> Far be it I should write thee sin, or blame,
> Or think thee unbefitting holiest place."
>   P. L. iv. 744. &c.

If it was not unworthy of the Paradise in which man was placed at creation, how should it be unworthy, when exalted to the same degree of purity as creation appointed for it, of the Paradise to which man is to be restored by redemption? If man is a real man after death; and if, as we have now seen, the origin of the distinction of sex is in the spirit; it necessarily follows, that human beings in the eternal world, are male and female still; and if so, that there are unions between them. On the whole: If the plain testimony of Scripture, the most obvious deductions of reason, and the most decided convictions of the intelligent and pious, be sufficient to determine this question, no question, it appears, can be more conclusively decided."*

Marriages in the heavens differ from marriages on earth, in this respect, that marriages on earth are for the additional purpose of the procreation of offspring, but not in the heavens; for in the heavens, in the place of such procreation, there is the procreation of good and of truth. The reason why this latter procreation is instead of the former, is, because there, marriage is the marriage of good and of truth, as was shewn above; and in that marriage good and truth, and their conjunction, are loved above all things; therefore these are the principles which are propagated from marriages in the heavens. Hence it is that by nativities and generations in the Word, are signified spiritual nativities and generations, which are those of good and of truth: by sons and daughters, the truths and goods which are procreated; and by sons-in-law and daughters-in-law, their conjunctions, and so forth. From these considerations it is evident, that marriages in the heavens are not like marriages in the world, being spiritual in the heavens, which ought not be called marriages, but

---

* See "AN APPEAL IN BEHALF OF THE VIEWS," &c.

conjunctions of minds derived from the marriage of
good and truth; but on earth they are marriages,
because they are not only of the spirit, but also of
the flesh: And since there are no marriages of this
description in the heavens, therefore two conjugial
partners there are not called husband and wife; but
the conjugial partner of another is called (from the
angelic idea of the conjunction of two minds into
one,) by an expression, which signifies that each is
mutually the other's. Genuine conjugial love cannot possibly exist but between two, that is, in the
marriage of one man and of one wife; and in no
wise between more together, by reason that conjugial love is mutual and reciprocal, and the life of
one conjugial partner is in that of the other reciprocally, so as to form as it were ONE: such union
may exist between two, but not between more, inasmuch as more divide asunder that love. That a
christian, who marries more wives than one, com-
mits natural adultery, is agreeable to the Lord's
words, that it is not lawful to put away a wife, because from the beginning they were created to be
one flesh, and that he who putteth her away without just cause, and marrieth another, committeth
adultery; thus much more, he who doth not put
a wife away, but retaineth her, and superinduceth
another. This law, enacted by the Lord concerning
marriages, derives its internal ground from spiritual
marriage; for whatsoever the Lord spake in itself
was spiritual; which is meant by these words, "The

words which I speak unto you are spirit and are life," John vi. 63. The spirituality contained in it is this, that by polygamical marriage in the christian orb, the marriage of the Lord and the church is profaned; in like manner the marriage of good and of truth; and besides these, the Word, and with the Word, the church, and the profanation of those things is spiritual adultery. Moreover, good and truth, conjoined with an angel and a man, are not two but one, since in this case good is of truth and truth of good: this conjunction is as when man thinks what he wills, and wills what he thinks; in which case, thought and will make one—thus one mind, for thought forms, or exhibits in form, that which the will wills, and the will gives it delight; hence also it is, that two conjugial partners in heaven are not called two, but one angel. This also is what is meant by these words of the Lord, " Have ye not read, that He who made them from the beginning, made them male and female, and said, for this cause shall a man leave father and mother, and shall cleave to his wife, and they twain shall be one flesh; wherefore, they are no more twain, but one flesh; what, therefore, God hath joined together, let not man put asunder." Matt. xix. 4, 5, 6. In this passage is described the heavenly marriage in which the angels are, and at the same time the marriage of good and truth; and by man *not separating what God hath joined together*, is meant, that good ought not to be separated from truth. From these con-

F

siderations it is evident, that love truly conjugial is the union of two, as to the interiors, which are of thought and of will—thus which are of truth and of good, for truth is of the thought, and good is of the will: for he who is principled in love truly conjugial, loves what another thinks, and what another wills; thus also he loves to think as another, and loves to will as another, consequently to be united to another, and to become as one man. The delight of love truly conjugial, is an internal delight, because it is of minds; and it is also an external delight thence derived, which is of bodies; but the delight of love not truly conjugial, is only external delight without internal, which is that of bodies, not of minds; but this latter delight is terrestrial, nearly like that of the animals, and therefore in time perishes; but the former is celestial, such as that of men should be, and therefore it is permanent.

Conjugial Love.

" This love the sacred image bears
        Of heaven's Eternal King;
'Tis this His choicest blessing shares;
        From Him its beauties spring.
" In JESUS CHRIST, our God, we view
        Wisdom and love combin'd:
Of these, behold, an image true,
        The male and female mind!
" For male and female were design'd
        In union blest to meet:
Like love and wisdom in the mind;
        Like heav'nly light and heat."

SECTION VII.

SHEWING that by Marriage, in a more extensive sense, is to be understood the Conjunction of the Lord and the Church, as Husband and Wife.

" The marriage of the LAMB is come, and His WIFE hath made herself ready: blessed are they who are called unto the marriage supper of the LAMB." REV. xix. 7, 9.

THAT the Lord, in the Word, is called Bridegroom and Husband, and the church Bride and Wife, and that the conjunction of the Lord with the church, and the reciprocal conjunction of the church with the Lord, is called a Marriage, may appear from the following passages: " He who hath the BRIDE is the BRIDEGROOM, but the friend of the BRIDEGROOM, who standeth and heareth Him, rejoiceth with joy by reason of the BRIDEGROOM's voice," John iii. 29. These words were spoken by John the Baptist concerning the Lord. Again, " Jesus said, so long as the BRIDEGROOM is with them, the SONS OF THE NUPTIALS cannot fast; the days shall come when the BRIDEGROOM shall be taken away from them, and then shall they fast,"

Matt. ix. 15. Mark ii. 19, 20. Luke v. 34, 35. Again, " I saw the holy city New Jerusalem prepared as a BRIDE adorned for HER HUSBAND," Rev. xxi. 2. That by the New Jerusalem is meant the New Church of the Lord, shall be shewn hereafter. Again, " The angel said to John, Come, and I will shew thee the BRIDE THE LAMB'S WIFE, and he shewed him the holy city Jerusalem," Rev. xxi. 9, 10. Again, " The time of the MARRIAGE OF THE LAMB is come, and HIS WIFE hath made herself ready ; blessed are they who are called to the MARRIAGE SUPPER OF THE LAMB," Rev. xix. 7, 9. By the BRIDEGROOM, whom the five prepared virgins went forth to meet, and with WHOM they entered into the MARRIAGE, Matt. xxv. 1—10., is meant the Lord, as is evident from verse 13, where it is said, " Watch therefore, because ye know not the day, nor the hour, in which the SON OF MAN shall come." Not to mention many passages in the prophets.

It is in consequence of such marriage that the Lord is also called FATHER, and the church MOTHER, whence spiritual offspring is derived. That the Lord is called FATHER, appears from the following passages : " Unto us a child is born, unto us a son is given, and his name shall be called Wonderful, Counsellor, the Mighty God, FATHER OF ETERNITY, Prince of Peace," Isaiah ix. 5. Again, " Thou JEHOVAH art OUR FATHER, our REDEEMER from eternity is Thy name," Isa. lxiii. 16. Again, " Jesus said, Whoso seeth ME, seeth the FATHER who sent ME," John xii. 45. Again, " If ye have known ME, ye have known My FATHER also; and henceforth ye have known Him, and have seen Him," John xiv. 7. Again, " Philip said, Shew us the FATHER; Jesus said unto him, Whoso seeth ME, seeth the FATHER; how sayest thou then, shew us the FATHER?" John xiv, 8, 9. Again, " Jesus said, The FATHER and· I are ONE," John x. 30. Again, " All things that the FATHER hath are MINE," John xvi. 13. chap. xvii. 10. Again, " The FATHER is in ME, and I IN THE FATHER," John x. 38. chap. xiv. 10, 11, 20. That the Lord and His Father are one, as soul and body are one, and that God the Father descended from heaven, and assumed the human nature or principle, to redeem and save men, and that this human nature or principle is what is called Son, and said to be sent into the world, hath been fully shewn in the small work " CONCERNING THE LORD."

That the Church is called MOTHER, appears from the following passages : " Jehovah said, Contend with YOUR MOTHER, she is not My WIFE, and I am not her HUSBAND," Hosea ii. 2, 5. Again, " Thou art thy MOTHER's daughter, that loatheth her HUSBAND," Ezek. xvi. 45. Again, " Where is the bill of thy MOTHER's divorcement, whom I have put away," Isa. l. 1. Again, " Thy MOTHER was as a vine planted near waters, bearing fruit," Ezek. xix. 10. speaking of the Jewish Church. Again,

" Jesus, stretching out His hand to the disciples, said, MY MOTHER and My brethren are they who hear the Word of God and do it," Luke viii. 21. Matt. xii. 48, 49. Mark iii. 33, 34, 35. By the Lord's disciples is meant the church. Again, " There was standing at the cross of Jesus, His mother; and Jesus, seeing His mother and the disciple standing by, whom He loved, saith to His mother, Woman, behold thy son; and He saith to the disciple, Behold thy mother; wherefore, from that hour the disciple took her into his own (*in propria*)," John xix. 25, 26, 27. By these words is implied, that the Lord did not acknowledge Mary as a mother, but the church, wherefore he calls her woman, and the mother of the disciple; the reason why the Lord called her the mother of the disciple, or of John, was, because John represented the church as to the goods of charity, which goods are the church in real effect; therefore it is said, that he took her into his own. That Peter represented truth or faith, James charity, and John the works of charity; and that the twelve disciples together, represented the church, as to all and singular things, may be seen in the APOCALYPSE REVEALED.

That no other than spiritual offsprings are born of the Lord by the church, is a proposition which wants no demonstration; because reason sees it to be self-evident; for it is the Lord from whom every good and truth proceeds; and it is the church which receives those principles, and brings them into effect; and

all the spiritual things of heaven and of the church
have relation to good and truth; hence it is that by
sons and daughters in the, Word, in its spiritual
sense, are meant truths and goods; by sons, truths
conceived in the spiritual man, and born in the natural; and by daughters, goods in like manner;
wherefore they who are regenerated of the Lord,
are called in the Word sons of God, sons of the
kingdom, born of Him, and the Lord called the disciples sons; by the male birth, whom the woman
brought forth, and who was caught up to God, Rev.
xii. 5. nothing else is signified. Inasmuch as by daughters are signified goods of the church, therefore in
the Word, mention is so frequently made of the
daughter of Zion, the daughter of Jerusalem, the
daughter of Israel, and the daughter of Judah; by
whom is signified, not any daughter, but the affection of good, which is an affection of the church.
The Lord also calls those brethren and sisters, who
are of His Church; see Matt. xiii. 49.; xxv. 40.;
xviii. 10. Mark iii. 35. Luke viii. 21.

The ground and reason why truths and goods are
the spiritual offsprings, which are born of the Lord
by the church, is, because the Lord is essential
good and essential truth, and these principles in
Him, are not two but one; also, because nothing
else can proceed from the Lord but what is in
Him, and what He is; and the reason why man
receives truth by virtue of the good and truth which
proceed as one from the Lord, is, because he receives this as his own, and appropriates it to him-

self as his own, for he thinks what is true as from
himself, and in like manner speaks from what is
true; and this effect hath place, because truth is in
the light of the understanding, and hence he sees
it; and whatsoever he sees in himself, or in his
mind, he knows not whence it is, for he doth not
see the influx, as he sees those objects which strike
upon the bodily vision; hence he supposes that it is
in himself. That it should appear thus, is granted
of the Lord to man, in order to his being man, and
that he may have a reciprocal principle of conjunction. Add to this, that man is born a faculty of
knowing, of understanding, and of growing wise,
and this faculty receives truths, whereby it hath
science, intelligence, and wisdom; and whereas the
female was created by the truth of the male, and is
formed into the love thereof more and more after
marriage, it follows, that she also receives the husband's truth in herself, and conjoins it with her own
good. And the reason why the Lord adjoins and
conjoins good to the truths which man receives, is,
because man cannot take good as of himself, it being
no object of his sight, inasmuch as it doth not appertain to light, but to heat, and heat is felt and not
seen : wherefore, when man sees truth in his thinking principle, he seldom reflects upon the good which
flows into it from the love of the will-principle, and
which gives it life. Neither doth a wife reflect upon
the good appertaining to her, but upon the husband's
inclination towards her, which inclination is according to the ascent of his understanding to wisdom;

the good which appertains to her from the Lord,
she applies without the husband knowing any thing
respecting such application. From these considerations then, it manifestly appears, that man receives
truth from the Lord, and that the Lord adjoins
good to that truth, according to the application of
truth to use, consequently, as man is desirous to
think wisely, and thence to live wisely.

It is in this manner that the church is formed
with man from the Lord, and the reason why it is
thus formed, is, because in such a case man is in
conjunction with the Lord, in good from Him, and
in truth as from himself; thus man is in the Lord
and the Lord in him, according to the Lord's words
in John xv. 4, 5. The case is the same, if, instead
of good we say charity, and instead of truth, faith;
because good is of charity, and truth is of faith. It
is well to be observed, however, that the church
hath place with those only, who come to the Lord,
and live according to His precepts; and the reason
why it hath place with those only, who come to
Him, is, because His Church, in that part of the
globe which is called christian, is derived from the
Word, and the Word is from Him, and in such a
manner from Him, that it is He Himself, the Divine
Truth being therein united to the Divine Good, and
this also is the Lord; nothing else is meant by the
Word which was with God, and which was God,
from which men have life and light, and which was
made flesh, John i. 1—14.; and further, the ground

and reason why the church hath place with those only who come to Him, is, because it hath place with those only who believe in Him; for to believe that He is God the Saviour and Redeemer, that He is Jehovah our righteousness (justice), that He is the door by which we are to enter into the sheepfold, that is, into the church; that He is the Way, the Truth, and the Life, and that no one cometh to the Father but by Him; that the Father and He are one, besides many other particulars which He Himself teaches: to believe these things, I say, is impossible for any one to do, except by influence from Him; and the reason why this is impossible, unless He be approached and applied to, is, because He is the God of heaven and earth, as He also teaches; and who else is to be approached and applied to? and who else can be? The ground and reason why the church hath place with those who live according to His precepts, is, because there is conjunction with none else, for He saith, " He that hath My precepts, and doeth them, He it is that loveth Me, and I will love Him, and will make My abode with Him; but he who doth not love Me, doth not keep My precepts," John xiv. 21—24; love is conjunction, and conjunction with Lord is the church: hence it is that in the Word, in the spiritual sense, heaven and the church are understood by nuptials and marriages; and that hell, and the rejection of all things of heaven and the church, are understood by adulteries and whoredoms.

The reason why adulteries are held less in abhorrence with christians than with the gentiles, yea, than with some of the barbarous nations, is, because in the Christian world, at this day, there is not the marriage of good and truth, but the marriage of evil and the false; for the religion and doctrine of faith, separated from charity or good works, is a religion and doctrine of truth separated from good; and truth separated from good is not truth, but, interiorly looked into, is evil: hence there is in the christian religion at this day a doctrine of the false and evil, from which origin flow in the lust and favour of adultery from hell; and hence it is, that adulteries are believed to be allowable, and are practised without shame in the christian world: for, as hath been said above, the conjunction of evil and the false is spiritual adultery, from which, according to correspondence, exists natural adultery: From this circumstance it is, that adulteries and whoredoms, in the Word, signify the adulterations of good and falsifications of truth: hence it is, that Babylon is called the whore in the Apocalypse; likewise that Jerusalem is so called in the Word of the Old Testament; and that the Jewish nation was called by the Lord an adulterous nation, and from their father, the devil.

He who abstains from adulteries from any other motive than because they are sins, and against God, is still an adulterer; as for instance, if any one abstaineth from them for fear of the civil law and its

punishment; from fear of the loss of fame, and thence
of honour; from fear of diseases arising from them;
from fear of upbraidings at home from his wife, and
thence of tranquillity of life; from fear of chastise-
ments from the servants of the injured husband;
from poverty or from avarice; from any infirmity
arising either from abuse, or from age, or from impotence, or from disease; nay, if he abstain from
them on account of any natural or moral law, and
doth not abstain from them at the same time on account of the divine law, he is nevertheless interiorly
unchaste, and an adulterer; for he, notwithstanding,
believeth that they are not sins, and thence declar-
eth them lawful in his spirit, and thereby in spirit
committeth them, although not in the body; wherefore, after death, when such a one becometh a spirit, he speaketh openly in favour of them, and committeth them without shame. It hath been given
me in the spiritual world to see virgins who accounted whoredoms as wicked, because against the
divine law; and also virgins who did not account
them wicked, but nevertheless abstained from them,
by reason of the ill fame attending them, which
would turn away their suiters: these latter virgins
I saw encompassed with a dusky cloud in their de-
scent to the abodes below; but the former I saw
encompassed with a bright light in their ascent to
the abodes above.

SECTION VIII.

*Shewing that by Marriage, in the supreme sense, is
to be understood the union of the Lord's Divinity
with His Humanity, or the Divine Good with
the Divine Truth, which the Lord fully
perfected in Himself while in the world.*

" And God said, Let us make man in our image, after our likeness: so God created man in His own image, in the image of God
created He him; male and female created He them."* Gen. i. 26, 27.

" That they may be one, even as we are one." John xvii. 22.

In Jehovah, or the Lord, there is nothing but what
is infinite, and inasmuch as it is infinite, it cannot

---

* How plain it is from this passage, in which we are express-
ly told, that man was created in the *image of God*, and yet
was created *male and female*, to see that there is a DUALITY
of character in the Divine Being, corresponding to the two-
fold character of male and female into which the human race
at large is divided! Hence also it may be seen, that these
must be united in pairs, that man may resemble God, or *again*
become an *image of God* from which he had fallen, but to
which he is restored by means of the heavenly marriage or regeneration. When therefore these two principles or characters
are united, they necessarily produce a *third*, which with man
is *spiritual offspring* or *use*, but with the Lord, the *Holy Spirit*
or *Divine Operation*. See John viii. 29.; chap. xx. 22. Psa.
xxxiii. 6.

G

be apprehended by any idea only as being the Esse
and Existere of all Good and Truth, or essential
Good and essential Truth; essential Good is the
Father, and essential Truth is the Son; and whereas there is a divine marriage or union of Good with
Truth, and of Truth with Good, therefore the Father
is in the Son, and the Son in the Father, as the Lord
Himself teaches in John, " Jesus said to Philip,
believest thou not THAT I AM IN THE FATHER, AND
THE FATHER IN ME," xiv. 10, 11.; and again, in
the same Evangelist, Jesus said to the Jews, " If ye
believe not Me, believe the works, that ye may
know and believe that THE FATHER IS IN ME, AND
I IN THE FATHER," x. 38.; and again, " I pray for
them, for all MINE ARE THINE, AND THINE ARE
MINE, that they all may be one, as THOU FATHER ART
IN ME, AND I IN THEE," xvii. 9, 10, 21.; and again,
" Now is the Son of man glorified, and God is glorified in Him; if God be glorified in Him, God shall also
glorify Him in Himself:" "FATHER, GLORIFY THY
SON, THAT THY SON ALSO MAY GLORIFY THEE," xiii.
31, 32.; chap. xvii. 1. Hence it may appear what is
the nature of the union of the Divine Principle and
the Human in the Lord, viz. that it is a mutual or
reciprocal union, which union is what is called the
Divine Marriage, from which descends the heavenly
marriage, which is the Lord's essential kingdom in
the heavens, concerning which the Lord thus speaks
in John, " In that day ye shall know that I am in my
Father, and YE IN ME, AND I IN YOU," xiv. 20.: and

again, "I pray for them, that they all may be one, as THOU FATHER ART IN ME AND I IN THEE, that they also may be one in us; I IN THEM, AND THOU IN ME; that THE LOVE with which Thou hast loved Me, MAY BE IN THEM, AND I IN THEM," xvii. 21, 22, 22, 23, 26.: That this heavenly marriage is the marriage of Good and Truth, and of Truth and Good is very evident. And whereas Divine Good can in no wise be and exist without Divine Truth, nor Divine Truth without Divine Good, but one is in the other mutually and reciprocally, it is hence manifest, that the Divine Marriage was from eternity, that is, the Father in the Son, and the Son in the Father, as the Lord Himself teaches in John, "And now, O Father, glorify thou Me with thine own Self, with the glory which I had with Thee before the world was," xvii. 5, 24.; but the Divine Truth or Son, which was born from eternity, was also born in time, and what was born in time, and glorified, is the same; hence it is, that the Lord so often said, that He went to the Father who sent Him, that is, that He returned to the Father; and in John, "In the beginning was the Word, (the Word is essential Divine Truth,) and the Word was with God, and God was the Word; the same was in the beginning with God; all things were made by Him, and without Him was not any thing made that was made: And the Word was made FLESH, and dwelt among us, and we saw His glory—the glory as of the only-begotten of the Father, full of grace and

TRUTH," i. 1, 2, 3, 14. : See also John iii. 13. chap. vi. 62.

From what has been now said and shewn, it must be evident that marriage, in the supreme sense, is the union of the Divine Itself, with the Divine Human in the Lord, or of Divine Good (which is the Father), with Divine Truth (which is the Son), and that it is this union which makes HEAVEN; for what proceeds from the Lord is divine truth from divine good, hence heaven is heaven, and is called a MARRIAGE; for the conjunction of Good and Truth there, which proceeds from the Lord, is what constitutes it; and whereas the Lord is the Good there, and heaven is the Truth thence derived, therefore the Lord in the Word is called Bridegroom, and heaven and also the church is called the Bride, for Good and Truth make a marriage, and their conjunction is what is meant by the conjugial principle. Hence it may be evidently concluded, that man, if he expects heaven, must not only be in the truth which is of faith, but also in the good which is of charity, and that otherwise there is no heaven in him.

But this subject is capable of still further confirmation from the particular style in which the Word is written, which, being one and the same with its Divine Author, is the Divine Prototype of the heavenly marriage. That the marriage of the Lord and His Church, and consequently the marriage of good and truth, is in every part of the

Word, hath never yet been discoved by mortal eyes, nor could it be discovered, so long as the spiritual sense of the Word remained unknown, inasmuch as it is this sense alone that can make manifest such a marriage. For there are two senses contained in the Word, which lie concealed in its literal sense, and which are called spiritual and celestial; what belongeth to the spiritual sense of the Word, hath relation to the church, and what belongeth to the celestial sense of the Word, hath relation to the Lord; the contents also of the spiritual sense have relation to Divine Truth, and the contents of the celestial sense, to Divine Good; and this is the ground of the above-mentioned marriage in the literal sense of the Word. But this is only apparent to those, who, by virtue of the spiritual and celestial sense of the Word, are acquainted with the significations of its names and expressions; for some particular expressions are predicated of Good, and some of Truth, and some include both; wherefore, without the knowledge of such significations it is impossible to see how such a marriage existeth in every part of the Word, and this is the reason why this *arcanum* was never heretofore discovered.

Inasmuch as such a marriage existeth in every part of the Word, therefore, we frequently find in the Word two expressions which appear like repetitions of one and the same thing; whereas they are not repetitions, but one hath relation to good, and the other to truth, and both taken together effect the conjunction of good and truth, and consequently make them one. This is the true ground of the divine sanctity of the Word; for in every divine word there is a conjunction of good with truth, and truth with good. The reason why we assert the marriage of good and truth in the Word, to be a consequence of the marriage of the Lord and the church therein, is, because wherever the marriage of the Lord and the church is, there also is the marriage of good and truth, inasmuch as the latter marriage is derived from the former; for whilst the church, or any of its members, are under the influence, and in the possession of truths, then the Lord, by virtue of His influencing Good, enters into those truths, and communicates life to them; or, what amounts to the same thing, whilst any member of the church is in the understanding of truth, then the Lord, by influx of the good of charity, enters into that understanding, and thereby communicates life to it.

That there are two expressions used in the Word, which appear like repetitions of the same thing, must be evident to every attentive reader; as, for instance, brother and companion, poor and needy, wilderness and desert, vanity and emptiness, enemy and adversary, sin and iniquity, anger and wrath, nation and people, joy and gladness, mourning and weeping, justice and judgment, &c. &c. which appear to be synonymous expressions, when in fact they are not: for the terms, brother, poor, wilderness, vanity, enemy, sin, anger, nation, joy, mourning, and justice, are predicated of Good, and in the opposite sense of evil; whereas the terms, companion, needy, desert, emptiness, adversary, iniquity, wrath, people, gladness, weeping and judgment, are predicated of Truth, and in the opposite sense of the false; yet it must appear to the reader, who is unacquainted with this *arcanum*, as if the terms, poor and needy, wilderness and desert, vanity and emptiness, &c. &c. were one and the same thing, whereas they are not so, yet become one thing by conjunction. In the Word also, we frequently find two things joined, as fire and flame, gold and silver, brass and iron, wood and stone, bread and water, bread and wine, purple and fine linen, &c.; because fire, gold, brass, wood, bread, purple, are predicated of Good, and flame, silver, iron, stone, water, wine, and fine linen, are predicated of Truth. In like manner it is said, that God is to be loved with all the heart, and with all the soul, and also, that God will create in man a new heart, and a new spirit; for heart is predicated of the good of love, and soul and spirit of the truth of faith. There are some expressions likewise, which, in consequence of partaking alike both of good and truth, are used singly by themselves, without the adjunction of others; but these, and many things besides, are known only to the angels, and to those who see into the spiritual sense of the Word, whilst they are reading the natural sense.

By reason of the marriage of the Lord with the church, or what amounts to the same thing, by reason of the marriage of Divine Good with Divine Truth in every part of the Word, there is frequent mention made of Jehovah and God, and also of Jehovah and the Holy One of Israel, as if they were two, when nevertheless they are one; for by Jehovah is meant the Lord with respect to the Divine Good of His Divine Love, and by God and the Holy One of Israel, is meant the Lord with respect to the Divine Truth of His Divine Wisdom. Divine Good is in the Lord, thus is His Esse, which in the Word is called Jehovah; but Divine Truth is from the Lord, —thus is the Existere from that Esse, which Existere in the Word is meant by the term God; and because this which exists from Him, is also Him, therefore also the Lord is the Word or Divine Truth, which is His Divine Principle, both in the heavens and in the church; for the heavens as well as the church exist from Him by means of the Word or Divine Truth, agreeable to these words, " By THE WORD OF THE LORD were the heavens made; and all the host of them by the breath of His mouth," Ps. xxxiii. 6.; again, " Man shall not live by bread only, but by EVERY WORD THAT PROCEEDETH OUT OF THE MOUTH OF GOD," Deut. viii. 3. Matt. iv. 4. Luke iv. 4.

That such a marriage as we have been describing, is in every part of the Word, may most manifestly appear from the internal sense of the two

names of our Lord, JESUS CHRIST: When these
names are pronounced, few have any other idea,
than that they are proper names, and almost like
the names of another man, but more holy; the
learned indeed know, that JESUS signifies Saviour,
and CHRIST the Anointed, and hence they conceive
some more interior idea; but still this is not what
the angels in heaven perceive from those names,
their perceptions extending to things still more divine, for by JESUS, when the name is pronounced
by man in reading the Word, they perceive the Divine Good, and by CHRIST, the Divine Truth, and
by BOTH, the Divine Marriage of Good and Truth,
and of Truth and Good, consequently all that is
Divine in the heavenly marriage, which *is* heaven.
These are the perceptions which the angels have,
when the name Jesus Christ is pronounced, and
this is what is signified when it is said, that *there is*
salvation in no other NAME; this also is signified by
what the Lord so often said concerning His Name,
as in John, " Whatsoever ye shall ask in MY NAME,
I will do," xiv. 13, 14.; Again, in the same Evangelist, " These things are written that ye may believe that JESUS is the CHRIST the Son of God, and
that believing ye may have life in HIS NAME," xx.
31.; and in other places: for NAME denotes every
thing in one complex, whereby the Lord is worshipped, consequently the quality of all worship and
doctrine; in the present case, therefore, it denotes
the good of love and of charity, conjoined with the

truth of faith, which is the complex of all doctrine
and of all worship.

In the Word throughout, mention is made in
one series of kings and priests, also of kings, princes,
priests, and prophets ; but in such passages, in the
internal sense, by *kings* are signified truths in the
complex, by *princes* primary truths, by *priests* goods
in the complex, and by *prophets* doctrines ; as in the
Revelation, " Jesus Christ hath made us *kings* and
priests," i. 6.; v. 10. : and in Jeremiah, "The house
of Israel were ashamed, themselves, their *kings*,
their *princes*, and their *priests*, and their *prophets*,"
ii. 26. : again, " In that day *the heart of the king*
shall perish, and *the heart of the princes*, and the
priests shall be amazed, and the *prophets* shall wonder," iv. 9.; thus by kings in the sense abstracted
from persons, are signified truths in the complex ; by
princes, primary truths; by priests, goods; and by
prophets, doctrines derived from them, and concerning them.   Moreover the Regal (office or character)
of the Lord is also signified by His name Christ,
inasmuch as Christ and Messiah are the same, and
Christ in the Greek tongue, and Messiah in
the Hebrew, signifies Anointed, which is the
same as King; and His Priestly (office or character) by His name JESUS, for Jesus signifies Saviour or Salvation, concerning which it is thus written in Matthew, " The angel appearing in sleep to
Joseph, said, thou shalt call HIS NAME JESUS, because HE SHALL SAVE His people from their sins,"

i. 21. and in consequence of such signification, it signifies Divine Good, inasmuch as all salvation is from Divine Good, which is of the Lord's Love and Mercy, and thus by the reception thereof; and inasmuch as this was of the Priesthood, therefore the like was represented by the office of the high priest expiating the people from sins, Levit. iv. 26, 31, 35.; v. 6, 10, 13, 16, 18.; ix. 7.; xv. 15, 30.

With respect to the name CHRIST which is the same as Messiah, Anointed, and King, signifying Divine Truth, the Lord also Himself teacheth this in John, " Pilate said to Jesus, art THOU A KING then? Jesus answered, Thou sayest that I AM A KING: For this was I born, and for this came I into the world, that I might bear witness unto THE TRUTH. Every one that is of THE TRUTH, heareth My voice," xviii. 37. whence it is manifest, that the essential Divine Truth is that principle by virtue whereof the Lord was called King. The ground and reason why kings were to be anointed, and were thence called the anointed, was, because OIL, wherewith they were anointed, signified GOOD, as is evident from the parable of the ten virgins, not to mention other instances, denoting that truth, which was signified by king, was from good, consequently the truth of good, and thus the Royalty appertaining to kings, represented the Lord as to Divine Truth, grounded in Divine Good, consequently the Divine Marriage of Good in Truth; whereas the Priesthood represented the Divine Marriage of Truth in

Good; the latter is signified by JESUS, the former by CHRIST. Hence it is evident, what is signified by *Christs* in these words of the Lord in Matthew, " See that no one seduce you ; for many shall come in My name, saying, I am *Christ*, and shall seduce many. Then, if any one shall say to you, Lo, here is *Christ*, or there, believe not, for there shall arise *false Christs*, and false prophets," xxiv. 5, 23, 24.; by false Christs are here signified, truths not Divine, or falses, and by false prophets, they who teach them. Again, in the same Evangelist, " Be ye not called Masters, for one is your Master, even CHRIST," xxiii. 10. where Christ denotes Truth Divine. Hence also it is evident what is meant by a Christian, viz. one who is in truth grounded in good.

From what hath been said, it may appear, how many hidden things are contained in the Word, which can in no wise come to any one's knowledge, except from the internal sense; as for instance, that the Word is the perfect marriage of Good and Truth ; and is, as to its literal sense, a DIVINE MEDIUM of conjunction with the Lord, and of consociation with the angels of heaven ; and inasmuch as it is from the Lord, and what is from the Lord, is also Himself, it follows, that whilst man reads the Word, and collects truths out of it, the Lord adjoins good; for man doth not see the goods which affect him in reading, because he reads the Word from the understanding, and the understanding imbibes thence only such things as are agreeable to its own nature, that is, truths. That good is adjoined thereto from the Lord, is made sensible to the understanding, from the delight which flows in, during a state of illustration; but this effect hath place interiorly with those only, who read the Word, to the end that they may become *wise*, and they are principled in this end of becoming wise, who are desirous of learning the genuine truths contained in the Word, and thereby forming of the church in themselves; whereas, they who read the Word, only with the view to gain the reputation of erudition, and they also who read it from an opinion that the mere reading or hearing inspires faith, and conduces to salvation, do not receive any good from the Lord, inasmuch as the end proposed by the latter, is to save themselves, by the mere expressions contained in the Word, uninfluenced by any principle of truth ; and the end proposed by the former, is to be distinguished for their learning, which end hath no conjunction with any spiritual good, but only with the natural delight arising from worldly glory. Inasmuch as the Word is the medium of conjunction, it is therefore called COVENANT, the old and the new, and covenant signifies conjunction.

As to what concerns the term Word, in the original tongue, it is expressive of THING; hence Divine Revelation is called the Word, and also the Lord in the supreme sense; and by the Word, when it is predicated of the Lord, and likewise of Revelation

from Him, in the proximate sense, is signified the
Divine Truth, from which all things, which are
things, exist.　That all things, which are things,
have existed, and do exist, by the Divine Truth
which is from the Lord, thus by the Word, is an arcanum which hath not as yet been discovered.
There are two things which proceed from the Lord,
divine love and divine wisdom, or, what is the same
thing, divine good and divine truth; for divine good
hath relation to the essential divine love, and divine
truth hath relation to the essential divine wisdom :
the Word in its essence is both of these principles;
and inasmuch as it effecteth conjunction between
man and the Lord, and openeth heaven, therefore,
when man readeth it under the Lord's influence, and
not under the influence of proprium or self-hood, it
replenisheth him with the good things of love and
the truths of wisdom—his will with the good things
of love, and his understanding with the truths of
wisdom; hence man hath life by and through the
Word.　Whosoever, therefore, reads the Word, to
the end that he may grow wise, that is, may do
what is good, and understand what is true, he is instructed according to such end and according to the
affection thereof; for the Lord flows in whilst he
knows not, and illuminates his mind, and wherein he
hesitates, gives understanding from other passages.
On this account every one, even at this day, who
goes to the Lord alone, whilst he reads the Word
and prays to Him, is enlightened in it.

When the Lord was in the world, and glorified His Human Principle, He first made it Divine Truth, and by degrees Divine Good of the Divine Love; and afterwards from the Divine Good of the Divine Love, He is operative in heaven and in the world, and gives them life, which is effected by the Divine Truth proceeding from Him; (see John xx. 22.(; for from it the heavens have existed, and from it they perpetually exist, that is, subsist. Now, whereas the Word is the Divine Wisdom of the Divine Love, it follows, that it is Jehovah Himself; thus the Lord, *by Whom all things are made that are made,* for from the Divine Love, by the Divine Wisdom, all things were created.

That it is the same Word which was manifested by Moses and the Prophets, and by the Evangelists, which is here specifically understood, may manifestly appear from this consideration, that it is the Divine Truth Itself from which the angels have all wisdom, and men spiritual intelligence; for it is the same Word which is with men in the world, and also with the angels in the heavens; but in the world with men it is *natural,* whereas in the heavens it is *spiritual;* and inasmuch as it is Divine Truth it is also the Divine Proceeding, and this not only is *from* the Lord, but also *is* the Lord Himself: And inasmuch as it is the Lord Himself, therefore, all and singular the things of the Word are written concerning Him alone; from Isaiah even to Malachi, there is not a single expression which does not treat of the Lord, or in the opposite sense of what is contrary to the Lord. That this is the case no one hath heretofore seen, but still every one may see it, if he only knows it, and whilst he reads, thinks it; and moreover knows that in the Word there is not only a natural sense, but also a spiritual sense, and that in this latter sense, by the names of persons and of places, is signified somewhat of the Lord, and hence somewhat of heaven and the church from Him, or something opposite. Inasmuch as all and singular the things of the Word are concerning the Lord, and the Word is the Lord, because it is Divine Truth, it is evident why it is said, " And the Word was made flesh, and dwelt among us, and we saw His glory, the glory as of the only begotten of the Father, full of grace and truth." Also why it is said, " Whilst ye have the light, believe in the light, that ye may be the children of the light;" again, " I am come a light into the world; he who abideth in Me doth not abide in darkness;" Light is Divine Truth, thus the Word.

Concerning the Divine Truth, scarce any one hath any other idea than as concerning a word which flows from the mouth of a speaker, and is dissipated in the air; this idea concerning the Divine Truth hath produced the opinion, that by the Word is meant only a command, and thereby that all things were created by God's saying and commanding, as a king in his kingdom; thus not from any real substance or thing which proceeds from the Lord; when yet truth and good are the principles of all things in both worlds—the spiritual and the natural; by which principles the universe was created, and by which the universe is preserved; and likewise by which man was made: wherefore those two principles are all in all. That the universe was created by Divine Truth, is plainly said in John, " In the beginning was the Word, and the Word was with God: all things were made by Him." And in David, " By the Word of Jehovah were the heavens made;" Ps. xxxiii. 6. By *the Word* in both cases is meant the Divine Truth: thus the universe was not created from or out of *nothing*, according to the common idea; but from *something* real and substantial, and indeed the very very real and essential THING from which are all things.

Inasmuch as the universe was created by Divine Truth, therefore, also the universe is preserved by it; for as subsistence is perpetual existence, so preservation is perpetual creation. The reason why man was made by the Divine Truth, is because all things of man have reference to understanding and will, and the understanding is the receptacle of divine truth, and the will of divine good; consequently the human mind, which consists of those two principles, is nothing else but a form of divine truth and divine good spiritually and naturally organized. From these considerations it may now be manifest for what cause God, as the Word, came into the world,

and was made man, viz. that this was for the sake
of redemption; for on this occasion, God, by the Human Principle, which was Divine Truth, put on all
power, and cast down, subdued, and reduced under
His obedience, the hells which had grown up even
to the heavens, where the angels were, and this not
by an *oral word*, but by the Divine Word, which is
Divine Truth.

The Lord our Saviour is Jehovah the Father
Himself in a human form; for Jehovah descended
and was made man, that He might come to man and
man to Him, and thus conjunction might be effected, and by conjunction man might have salvation and
eternal life. In short the Lord our Saviour is the universal Heaven, as being the All therein : That from
Him is the All of Innocence, of Peace, of Love, of
Charity, of Mercy, of Conjugial Love, all Good and
all Truth: That Moses and the Prophets, consequently the Word in all its particulars, hath relation to
Him, and that all the rites of the Church represented Him. This now is the Lord, Who, as to the Divine Human, is the Alone Man, and from Whom
man hath what constitutes him man.

*Now to JESUS CHRIST be All Honour, and
Dominion, and Glory; for HE is ALPHA and
OMEGA, the BEGINNING and the ENDING,
the FIRST and the LAST, Who is, and Who was,
and Who is to come, the ALMIGHTY. Amen.*

ON THE

LIFE OF MAN AFTER DEATH.

———————

SECTION I.

Shewing that man after death is of a quality agreeable to that of his former life in the world.

———————

" He that is unjust, let him be unjust still; and he that is filthy, let him be filthy still; and he that is righteous, let him be righteous still; and he that is holy, let him be holy still: And, behold, I come quickly; and My reward is with Me, to give every man according as his work shall be. Amen, Even so come, Lord Jesus." REV. xxii. 11, 12, 20.

———————

THAT every one's life remains with him after death, is known to every christian from the Word; for it is there said, in many passages, that man will be judged and recompensed according to his deeds and works: every one also who thinks from a principle of good, and from essential truth, cannot see otherwise, than that he who lives well comes into heaven, and that he who lives wickedly comes into

hell: Nevertheless he who is principled in evil,
is not willing to believe that his state after death
is according to his life in the world; but thinks, especially in sickness, that heaven is open to every
one from pure mercy, whatsoever his life hath been,
and that it is according to faith, which he separates
from life.

That man will be judged and recompensed according to his deeds and works, is said in many passages
in the Word, some of which I shall here adduce:
" The Son of Man shall come in the glory of His
Father, with His angels, and shall then render to
every one according to his works," Matt. xvi. 17.:
" Blessed are the dead who die in the Lord; yea,
saith the Spirit, that they may rest from their labours,
and their works do follow them," Rev. xiv. 11.: " I
will give to every one according to his works," Rev.
ii. 23.: " I saw the dead, small and great, standing
before God, and the books were opened, and the
dead were judged according to those things that were
written in the books, according to their works: the
sea gave up those who were dead in it, and death
and hell gave up those who were in them; and they
were judged every one according to their works,"
Rev. xx. 13, 15.: " Behold I come, and My reward
is with Me, that I may give to every one according
to his works," Rev. xxii. 12.: " Every one who
heareth My words and doeth them, I will compare
to a prudent man; but every one who heareth My
words and doeth them not, is compared to a foolish

man," Matt. vii. 24, 26.: "Not every one that saith
to Me, Lord, Lord, shall enter into the kingdom of
heaven: many shall say unto Me in that day, Lord,
Lord, have we not prophesied in Thy name, and in
Thy name cast out demons, and in Thy name done
many wonderful works? And then will I profess
unto them, I never knew you, depart from Me ye
workers of iniquity," Matt. vii. 22, 23.: "Then
shall ye begin to say, we have eaten and drunk in
Thy presence, and Thou hast taught in our streets;
but He shall say, I tell you, I know you not,
ye workers of iniquity," Luke xiii. 26, 27.:
"I will recompense them according to their deeds,
and according to the works of their own hands,"
Jer. xxv. 14.: "Jehovah, whose eyes are open on
all the ways of man, to give every one according
to his ways, and according to the fruit of his doings,"
Jer. xxxii. 19. "I will punish them for their ways,
and reward them for their doings," Hosea iv. 9.
"Jehovah doeth with us according to our ways, and
according to our doings," Zech. i. 6. Where the
Lord predicts concerning the last judgment, He
recounts nothing but works, teaching that they
should enter into eternal life who had done good
works, and into damnation who had done evil works,
Matt. xxv. 32—46. Not to mention many other
passages, where the subject treated of is concerning
the salvation and condemnation of man. That works
and deeds are the external life of man, and that by

them his internal life is manifested as to its quality, is evident.

But by deeds and works are not understood deeds and works only, such as are presented in an external form, but also such as they are in the internal form; for every one knows that every deed and work proceeds from man's will and thought, since, if it did not proceed thence, it would be a mere motion, such as is that of an automaton and image; wherefore a deed or work, viewed in itself, is only an effect, which derives its soul and life from the will and thought, insomuch that it is will and thought in effect, consequently is will and thought in an external form: hence it follows, that such as the will and thought are, which produce a deed or work, such likewise is the deed and work; if the thought and will be good, in such case the deeds and works are good, but if the thought and will be evil, in such case the deeds and works are evil, although in the external form they appear alike : a thousand men may act alike, that is, may present a similar deed, so alike, that, as to the external form, they can scarce be distinguished, and yet each, viewed in itself, is dissimilar, because from dissimilar will: as, for example, in the case of acting sincerely and justly with a companion; one person may act sincerely and justly with him, to the intent that it may appear that he is sincere and just for the sake of himself and his own credit; another, for the sake of the world and of gain; a third, for the sake of recompense

and merit; a fourth, for the sake of friendship; a
fifth, on account of the fear of the law, of the loss
of reputation, and of employment; a sixth, to engage
another to his own party although it be evil; a seventh, to deceive; thus, others with other views and
purposes; but the deeds of all these, although they
appear good, since it is good to act sincerely and
justly with a companion, are still evil, inasmuch as
they are not done for the sake of what is sincere
and just, and out love to those principles, but for
the sake of self and the world, which are the objects
loved, and to which love, what is sincere and just
serves as servants to a lord, whom the lord despises
and casts off when they do not serve him. They
also act sincerely and justly with a companion in
like appearance as to the external form, who act
from the love of what is sincere and just, some of
them from the truth of faith, or from obedience,
because it is so commanded in the Word: some from
the good of faith, or from conscience, because from
religious principle; some from the good of charity
towards their neighbour, because his good ought to
be consulted; some from the good of love to the
Lord, because good ought to be done for the sake
of good, thus likewise, what is sincere and just, for
the sake of what is sincere and just, which principles they love, because they are from the Lord, and
because the divine principle proceeding from the
Lord is in them; and hence, when regarded in their
very essence, they are divine: the deeds, or works,

of these latter are interiorly good, wherefore also they are exteriorly good, for, as was said above, deeds, or works, are altogether of such a quality as the thought and will are from which they proceed, and without these principles they are not deeds and works, but only inanimate motions. From these considerations it is manifest what is meant by works and deeds in the Word.

Inasmuch as deeds or works are of the will and of the thought, therefore also they are of the love and the faith, consequently they are of such a quality as the love and faith are; for whether we speak of the love or the will of man, it is the same thing, for what a man loves, this he likewise wills, and what a man believes, this he likewise thinks; if man loves what he believes, in this case he likewise wills it, and, as far as he is able, doeth it: every one may know that love and faith are in the will and thought of man, and that they are not out of them, since the will is what is enkindled by love, and the thought is what is illustrated in matters of faith, wherefore none are illustrated, but those who can think wisely,* and according to illustration, they think truths and will truths, or, what is the same thing, they believe truths and love truths.

It is, however, to be noted, that will makes the man, and thought only so far as it proceeds from

* As to the sense in which the term *wisely* is here used, the Reader is referred to the note at page 14.

the will, and that deeds and works proceed from
both ; or, what is the same thing, that love makes
the man, and faith, only so far as it proceeds from
love, and that deeds and works proceed from both :
hence it follows, that the will or love is the very
man himself, for the things which proceed are of
that principle from which they proceed ; to proceed
is to be produced and presented in a suitable form,
that it may be apperceived and appear. From these
considerations, it may be manifest what faith is, separate from love, viz. that it is no faith, but only
science, which hath no spiritual life in it; in like
manner, what a deed or work is, without love, viz.
that it is not a deed or work of life, but a deed or
work of death, in which there is an apparent principle of life derived from the love of evil, and from
the faith of what is false; this apparent principle of
life is what is called spiritual death.

It is further to be noted, that in deeds or works,
the whole man is exhibited, and that his will and
thought, or his love and faith, which are his interiors, are not complete, until they are in deeds or
works, which are the exteriors of the man; for
these latter things are the ultimates in which the
former terminate, and without termination they are
as it were things incomplete, which do not as yet
exist, thus which are not as yet in the man : to
think and to will without doing, when ability is given, is like a principle of flame inclosed in a vessel,
which principle becomes extinct; it is also like seed

I

cast upon sand, which doth not grow up, but perishes with its prolific principle; whereas to think and to will, and thence to do, is like a principle of flame which dispenses heat and light all around; and it is like seed in the ground, which grows up into a tree or a flower, and gains existence. Every one may know, that to will, and not to do, when ability is given, is not to will; also that to love and not to do good, when ability is given, is not to love; thus that it is only to think that he wills and loves, consequently that it is thought separate, which vanishes and is dissipated: love and will is the very soul itself of a deed or work, forming its body in the sincere and just actions which the man doeth; the spiritual body, or the body of the spirit of man, is from no other source, that is, it is formed from no other principles than from those things which man doeth from his love or will;* in a word, all things of the man and of his spirit are in his deeds or works.

From these considerations, it may now be manifest what is meant by the life which remains with man after death, viz. that it is his love, and the faith thence derived, not only in potency, but also

---

* This hint of our Author starts a subject to the mind, no less important, than of new and curious consideration; wherefore, let all such as are in love with true beauty, be heedful what spirit they are of, or what the nature of the love is from which they act, as the *spiritual body* is formed accordingly.

in act; thus that it consists in deeds or works, because these contain in them all things of man's love
and faith.

It is the ruling love which remains with man after death, neither is it ever changed to eternity;
every one is influenced by several loves, but still
they all have reference to his ruling love, and make
one with it, or together compose it. All things of
the will, which agree with the ruling loves, are
called loves, because they are loved: these loves
are interior and exterior, there being some which
are immediately conjoined, and some which are
mediately conjoined; some which are nearer and
some which are more remote; and some which are
rendered subservient in various manners; all taken
together constitute as it were a kingdom: for such is
there arrangement with man, although man is utter-
ly unacquainted with that arrangement. Nevertheless something is manifested to him in the other
life; for according to their arrangement he hath an
extent of thought and of affection there, an extent
into heavenly societies, if the ruling love consists of
heavenly loves, but into infernal societies if the
ruling love consists of infernal loves.

But the things which have been hitherto said, affect only the thought of the rational man; and therefore to the intent that they may be presented to
apperception before the senses, I shall adduce some
experimental cases for their illustration. FIRST,
That man, after death, is his own love or his own

will. SECONDLY, that man remains to eternity, such as he is as to his will or ruling love. THIRD-LY, That the man who is principled in celestial and spiritual love, comes into heaven; and the man who is principled in corporeal and worldly love, without celestial and spiritual, into hell. FOURTHLY, That faith doth not remain with man, unless it be grounded in heavenly love. FIFTHLY, That it is love in act which remains, thus that it is the life of man.

I. *THAT man after death is his own love, or his own will*, hath been testified to me by manifold experience. The universal heaven is distinguished into societies according to the differences of the good of love; and every spirit who is elevated into heaven, and becomes an angel, is conveyed to the society where his love is; and when he comes thither, he is as with himself, and as at the house where he was as it were born; this the angel perceives, and is there consociated with his like: when he departs thence, and comes to another place, there is constantly something of resistance, attended with an affection of desire to return to his like, thus to his ruling love. In this manner consociations in heaven are effected: in like manner in hell, where also they are consociated according to loves contrary to heavenly loves. That man after death is his own love, may likewise be manifest from this consideration, that those things are then removed, and as it were taken away from him, which do not make one with his ruling love: if he be a good spirit, all things discordant or disagreeing are removed, and as it were taken away, and thus he is let into his own love; in like manner an evil spirit,—but with this difference, that from the latter, truths are taken away, whilst from the good spirit, falses are taken away, until at length each becomes his own love; this is effected when the man-spirit is brought into the third state, which will be treated of in what follows. When this effect takes place, he then turns his face constantly to his love, which he hath continually before his eyes, in whatsoever direction he turns himself.

All spirits may be led at pleasure, provided only they be kept in their ruling love; nor can they resist, howsoever they may be aware that this is the case, and think that they will resist: On several occasions the trial has been made, whether they can act in any respect contrary to it, but in vain: their love is as a bond, or as a rope, with which they are as it were tied round, by which they may be drawn, and from which they cannot loosen themselves. The case is similar with men in the world, who are also led by their own love, and by that love are led by others; but more so when they become spirits, because then it is not allowed to present to appearance any other love; and to assume a semblance of what is not properly their own. That the spirit of man is his ruling love, is made manifest in all conso-

ciation in the other life; for so far as any one
acts and speaks according to the love of another, so far the latter appears with a full, cheerful, lively countenance throughout; but so far as
any one acts and speaks contrary to his love, so
far his countenance begins to be changed, to be
obscured, and not to appear ; and at length it totally
disappears, as if he had not been there.   That this
is the case, I have often wondered at, because nothing of the kind can have place in the world; but
I have been told, that the case is similar with the
spirit in man, which, when it averts itself from
another, is no longer in the view of him.

That a spirit is his ruling love, was also made
evident from this consideration, that every spirit
seizes upon and appropriates to himself all things
which are in agreement with his love, and rejects
and alienates from himself all things which are not
in agreement.   The love of every one is like spongy
and porous wood, which imbibes such fluids as con-
duce to its vegetation, and repels all others ; and it
is like animals of every kind, which know their
proper food, and appetite those things which agree
with their nature, and hold in aversion those things
which disagree; for every love is willing to be
nourished by its own [principles and persuasions],
evil love by falses, and good love by truths.   Occasionally it hath been given me to see, that certain
simple good spirits were desirous to instruct the
evil in truths and goods, but that the latter fled

away far from the instruction; and, when they came to their own, seized with much pleasure on the falses which were in agreement with their love: also that good spirits discoursed with each other concerning truths, which were heard with gratification by the good who were present, but not attended to by the evil who were also present, and who seemed as if they did not hear.

In the world of spirits* appear ways, some leading to heaven, some to hell, every one to some society; good spirits go in no other ways than in those which lead to heaven, and to the society which is principled in the good of their own love; and they do not see the ways which are in another direction; and if they see them, they are still not willing to walk in them. Such ways in the spiritual world, are real appearances, which correspond to truths or falses; wherefore ways, in the Word, signify truths or falses. From these documents of experience, confirmation is given to what was before said from reason, viz. that every man after death is his own love, and his own will: it is said, " his own will," because the will of every one is his love.

II. *THAT man after death remains to eternity such as he is as to his will or ruling love*, hath also been

---

* For an explanation of what is meant by the *world of spirits*, see the note at page 33.

confirmed by abundant experience. It hath been
granted me to discourse with some who lived two
thousand years ago, and whose lives are described
in history, and hence made known; they were found
to be still like themselves, and altogether such as
they had been described; thus of the same quality
as to the love from which, and according to which,
their lives were formed. There were others who
lived seventeen hundred years ago, and were also
made known by history; and there were others who
lived four hundred years ago, and some three, and
so forth, with whom also it was granted to converse, and it was found that a similar affection still
prevailed amongst them, with no other difference
than that the delights of their love were turned into
such things as correspond.

It was said by the angels, that the life of the ruling
love is never changed with any one to eternity, inasmuch as every one is his own love; and therefore to
change it with a spirit would be to deprive him of his
life, or to extinguish it. They explained also the
reason, viz. that man, after death, can no longer be
reformed by instruction, as in the world, because
the ultimate plane, which consists of natural knowledges and affections, is then quiescent, and cannot
be opened, because it is not spiritual; and that upon
that plane, the interior things which are of the mind,
rest as a house on its foundation; and that hence it
is that man remains to eternity, such as the life of
his love had been in the world.

The angels wonder exceedingly that man is not aware that every one is of such a quality as his ruling love is, and that many believe that they may be saved by immediate mercy, and by faith alone, without any regard to the quality of the life; and that they do not know that divine mercy is mediate, and that it consists in being led by the Lord, both in the world and afterwards to eternity, and that they are led by His mercy who do not live in evil; and that neither do they know that faith is the affection of truth proceeding from the heavenly love which is from the Lord.

III. *THAT the man who is principled in celestial and spiritual love, comes into heaven, and the man who is principled in corporeal and worldly love, without celestial and spiritual, into hell,* might be made evident to me from all whom I saw taken up into heaven, and cast into hell : they who were taken up into heaven had been principled in celestial and spiritual love as to life ; but they who were cast into hell, had formed their lives from corporeal and worldly love. Celestial love consists in loving what is good, sincere, and just, because it is good, sincere, and just, and in doing accordingly, under the influence of that love; whence they derive the life of what is good, sincere, and just, which is celestial life. They who love those principles for the sake of those principles, and do them or live them, love also the Lord above all things, because those principles are from Him ; and they also love their neigh-

bour, because those principles are the neighbour
who ought to be loved; but corporeal love consists
in loving what is good, sincere, and just, not for the
sake of those principles, but for the sake of self, because to secure thereby reputation, honour, and gain ;
in which case they do not regard the Lord and
their neighbour in what is good, sincere, and just,
but themselves and the world, taking delight in
frauds, which fraud renders good evil, sincerity insincere, and justice unjust ; so that evil, insincerity,
and injustice, are principally loved.

Inasmuch as the love thus determines the life of
every one ; therefore all, as soon as they come after
death into the world of spirits, are explored as to
their quality, and are brought into connection with
those who are in similar love : they who are in heavenly love, with those who are in heaven ; and they
who are in corporeal love, with those who are in hell :
and likewise when they have passed through a first
and second state, they are so separated that they no
longer see each other, nor know each other ; for
every one becomes his own love, not only as to the
interiors which are of the mind, but also as to the
exteriors which are of the face, of the body, and of
the speech, since every one becomes an effigy of
his own love, even in externals : they who are
corporeal loves, appear gross, obscure, black, and
deformed ; but they who are heavenly loves, appear cheerful, bright, fair, and beautiful : they
are also altogether dissimilar as to their minds

and thoughts; they who are heavenly loves are intelligent and wise, but they who are corporeal loves are stupid, and like persons infatuated : they again who are in corporael love, see nothing in the light of heaven, which to them is thick darkness, whereas the light of hell, which is as light from burning coals (compared with the light of the noon-day sun), is to them as clear light; in the light of heaven also their interior sight is darkened, insomuch that they are insane, wherefore they shun it, and (as it were,) hide themselves in caves and caverns, at a depih according to the falses derived from evils prevalent with them ; but, on the other hand, they who are in heavenly love, the more interiorly or superiorly, that they come into the light of heaven, so much the more clearly do they see all things, and likewise all things more beautiful, and so much the more intelligently and wisely do they perceive truths.

They who are in corporeal love, cannot in any wise live in the heat of heaven, for the heat of heaven is heavenly love, but in the heat of hell, which is the love of exercising rage towards others who do not favour themselves ; contempt of others, enmity, hatred, revenge are the delights of their love, and when they are in those delights, they are in their life, not at all knowing what it is to do good to others from a principle of good, and for the sake of good, but only to do good from evil, and for the sake of evil. Neither can they who are in corporeal love respire in heaven; for when any evil spirit is conveyed thither, he draws his breath as one who is in an agony of pain; whereas they who are in heavenly love, respire the more freely, and live the more fully, in proportion as they are admitted more interiorly into heaven.

From these considerations it may be manifest, that celestial and spiritual love is heaven with man, because on that love are inscribed all things of heaven; and that corporeal and worldly love, without celestial and spiritual, are hell with man, because on those loves are inscribed all things of hell. Hence it is evident, that he who is principled in celestial and spiritual love, comes into heaven, and he who is principled in corporeal and worldly love, without celestial and spiritual, into hell.

IV. *THAT faith doth not remain with man if it be not grounded in heavenly love,* hath been made manifest to me by so much experience, that if all things were to be adduced which I have seen and heard on the subject, they would fill a volume: this I can testify, that there is no faith at all, neither can any be given, with those who are in corporeal and worldly love without celestial and spiritual, and that it is only science, or persuasion, that a thing is true, because it serves their love. Several of those who supposed that they had been in the faith, were brought to those who were in the faith, and on this occasion, when communication was given, they perceived that they had no faith at all; they confessed also, afterwards, that merely to believe what is true, and to believe the Word, is not faith, but to love truth from a principle of heavenly love, and to will and do it from interior affection. It was likewise shewn that their persuasion, which they called faith, was only like the light of winter, in which, because there is no heat, all things on the earth, being frozen up, are torpid, and are buried in snow; wherefore the light of persuasive faith with them, as soon as it is shone upon by the rays of the light of heaven, is not only extinguished, but also becomes as thick darkness, in which no one seeth himself; and on this occasion the interiors at the same time are so darkened, that they understand nothing at all, and at length grow insane from falses. Wherefore with such all the truths are taken away, which they had learned from the Word, and from the doctrine of the Church, and had called the truths of their faith, and in their place they are imbued with every false principle which is in agreement with the evil of their life: for all are let into their own loves, and with them into concordant falses, and on this occasion they hate and hold in aversion, and thus reject truths, because they are repugnant to the falses of evil in which they are principled.

This I can testify from all my experience concerning the things of heaven and hell, that they who from doctrine have confessed faith alone, and have been in evil as to life, are all in hell. I have seen

K

them cast down thither, to the number of several thousands, of whom an account may be seen in a small work ON THE LAST JUDGEMENT.

V. *THAT love in act is what remains, thus that the life of man remains,* follows as a conclusion from what hath been just now shown from experience, and from what hath been above said concerning deeds and works ; love in act is work and deed.

It is to be noted, that all works and deeds are of moral and civil life, and hence that they regard what is sincere and right, also what is just and equitable; what is sincere and right is of moral life, and what is just and equitable is of civil life.   The love from which those principles are brought into effect, is either heavenly or infernal; works and deeds of moral and civil life are heavenly, if they are done from heavenly love, for the things done from heavenly love are done from the Lord, and the things done from the Lord are all of them good; but the deeds and works of moral and civil life are infernal, if they are done from infernal love, for the things done from this love, which is the love of self and of the world, are done from the man himself, and the things done from the man himself, are all in themselves evil : for man, viewed in himself, or his proprium, is nothing but evil.

SECTION II.

SHEWING that the Delights of the Life of every one after Death are turned into correspondent ones.

" Delight thyself also in the Lord, and He shall give thee the desires of thine heart." PSALM xxxvii. 4.

THAT the ruling affection, or predominant love, remains to eternity with every one, was shown in the preceding section; but that the delights of that affection or love are turned into correspondent ones, remains now to be shown. By being turned into correspondent ones, is meant, into spiritual delights, which are correspondent to natural : that they are turned into spiritual delights, may be manifest from this consideration, that man, so long as he is in his terrestrial body, is in the natural world; but when he leaves that body, he comes into the spiritual world, and puts on a spiritual body.

All the delights appertaining to man are of his ruling love; for man is not sensible of any other delight than of what he loves; thus he is most sensible of that which he loves above all things; for whether we speak of the ruling love, or of that which is loved above all things, it is the same thing.

Those delights are various; there are as many in
general as there are ruling loves, consequently as
many as there are men, spirits, and angels; for the
ruling love of one is not in every respect like that of
another; hence it is that no two faces are exactly
alike, for the face is an image of the mind of every
one, and in the spiritual world is an image of every
one's ruling love. The specific delights of every one
are also of infinite variety; nor is one delight of
any one like to or the same with another, whether they be regarded as succeeding one after another, or as abiding together one with the other;
for in neither case is one given the same with another; nevertheless these specific delights with every
one, have reference to his one love, which is the
ruling love, for they compose it, and thus make
one with it; in like manner all delights in general
have reference to one universally ruling love,—in
heaven, to love to the Lord, and in hell to the love
of self.

What and of what quality the spiritual delights are,
into which the natural delights of every one after
death are turned, cannot be known from any other
source than from the science of correspondences;
this science teacheth in general, that nothing natural is given which hath not something spiritual corresponding to it; and it also teacheth, specifically,
what and of what quality that is which corresponds;
wherefore, whosoever is principled in that science
may know his own state after death, provided he

only knows his own love, and what his quality is in the universally ruling love, to which all loves have reference, as was said just above. But to know the ruling love, is impossible for those who are principled in the love of self, because they love what is their own, and call their own evils goods, and at the same time call the falses or fallacies which favour them, and by which they confirm their own evils, truths; nevertheless, if they are willing, they may know it from others who are wise, since these see what they themselves do not see; but neither is this possible with those who are so intoxicated with the love of self, as to reject all teaching of those who are wise. But they who are principled in heavenly love, receive instruction, and see their own evils into which they were born, whilst they are betrayed into them, discerning them by virtue of truths, for these make evils manifest: for every one is capable, by virtue of truth which is derived from good, of seeing evil, and the false principle which attends it, but no one can see what is good and true from a principle of evil; the reason is, because the falses of evil are darkness, and likewise correspond to darkness, wherefore they who are principled in falses derived from evil, are as blind as persons who do not see the things which are in light,—they likewise shun them like birds of night: but truths derived from good are light, and likewise correspond to light; wherefore they who are in truths derived from good

K 2

are seers and persons whose eyes are open, and discern those things which are of light and of shade.

In what manner the delights of every one's life
are turned after death into corresponding delights,
may indeed be known from the science of correspondences; but inasmuch as that science is not as yet
made public, I shall endeavour to throw light on the
subject by some cases of experience.—All they who
are principled in evil, and have confirmed themselves in falses against the truths of the church, especially they who have rejected the Word, shun the
light of heaven, and plunge themselves into hiding-
places, which in the apertures appear extremely
dark, and into cliffs of rocks, where they hide themselves, and this because they have loved falses, and
have hated truths; for such hiding places, and likewise the cliffs of rocks, and also falses, correspond
to darkness, and light to truths; their delight is to
dwell there, and it is undelightful to them to dwell
in open plains. The case is similar with those who
have found delight in clandestine and insidious
purposes, and in the concealment of treacherous
designs; for they likewise conceal themselves in
those hiding-places, and enter into vaults which are
so obscure, that they cannot even see each other,
but whisper to each other in the corners; such is
the change of the delight of their love. They, again,
who have applied themselves to the study of the
sciences, without any other end than to acquire the
reputation of learning, and who have not cultivated

the rational principle by those sciences, and have hence, from self-conceit, taken delight in the things of memory, love sandy places, which they choose in preference to fields and gardens, because sandy places correspond to such studies. They, again, who have cultivated the science of the doctrinals of their own church, and of others, without any application of those doctrinals to life, choose for themselves craggy ground, where they dwell among heaps of stones, shunning places that are cultivated, because they hold them in aversion. They, again, who have ascribed all things to nature, and likewise they who have ascribed all things to their own prudence, and by various arts have raised themselves to honours, and have procured wealth, in the other life apply to the study of magical arts, which are abuses of divine order, in which they perceive the highest delight of life. They, again, who have applied divine truths to their own loves, and have thus falsified those truths, love urinous scents and matters, because urinous scents and matters correspond to the delights of such love. They, again, who have been sordidly avaricious, dwell in cells, and love such filth as swine delight in, and likewise substances which emit a stench such as is exhaled from indigested meat in the stomach. They, again, who have passed their lives in mere pleasure, living delicately, and indulging in the delights of appetite, so as to love them as the highest good of life, in the other life, love what is excrementitious, and the places in which it is deposited, which to them are objects of delight, by reason that such pleasures are spiritual filth; they shun clean places which are void of filth, because such places are undelightful to them. They, again, who have taken delight in adulteries, pass their time in brothels, where all things are dirty and filthy, loving such habitations, and shunning chaste houses, into which latter, when they enter, they fall into a swoon; nothing is more delightful to them than to break the bonds of marriage. They, again, who have been desirous of revenge, and have hence contracted a savage and cruel nature, love cadaverous substances, and likewise dwell in such hells. So in others instances.

But the delights of the life of those who, in the world, have lived in heavenly love, are turned into things corresponding, such as are in the heavens, which exist from the sun of heaven, and from the light thence derived, which light presents to view such things as inwardly conceal in them things divine; the objects which thence appear, affect the interiors of the angels which are of their minds, and at the same time the exteriors which are of their bodies; and whereas divine light, which is the divine truth proceeding from the Lord, flows in into their minds, which are opened by heavenly love, therefore, in externals it presents such things as correspond to the delights of their love: for those things which appear visible in the heavens, correspond to the interiors of the angels, or to those things which are of faith and love, and hence of their intelligence and wisdom. But inasmuch as we have undertaken to confirm this matter from cases of experience, in order to illustrate what hath been said above as to the causes of things, I feel disposed also to adduce some particulars concerning the heavenly delights into which natural delights are changed, with those who live in the world under the influence of heavenly love.

They who have loved divine truths and the Word from interior affection, or from the affection of truth itself, in the other life dwell in light, in elevated places, which appear as mountains, and are there continually in the light of heaven; they do not know what darkness like that of the night in the world is, and they likewise live in a vernal temperature; fields and crops of corn, as it were, and likewise vineyards, are presented to their view; in their houses, singular things are refulgent, as if they were of precious stones; when they look out through their windows, it is as if they looked through pure chrystal: these are the delights of their sight, and the same things are interiorly delightful from correspondence with divine-celestial things, for the truths derived from the Word, which they have loved, correspond to crops of corn, to vineyards, to precious stones, to windows and chrystals. They, again, who have immediately applied to life the doctrinals of the church derived from the Word, are in the inmost heaven, and excel all others in the de-

light of wisdom : in singular objects they see things
divine ; they see indeed the objects, but the corresponding divine things flow in immediately into their
minds, and fill them with blessedness, with which
all their sensations are affected, hence all things, as
it were, laugh, sport, and live before their eyes.
They, again, who have loved the sciences, and by
them have cultivated their rational principle, and
have thence procured to themselves intelligence,
and at the same time have acknowledged a Divine
Being or Principle, experience in the other life a
change of the pleasure of the sciences, and of rational
delight, into spiritual delight, which is that of the
. knowledges of good and truth ; they dwell in gardens, where there appear beds of flowers, and grass
plots beautifully arranged, and rows of trees round
about with porticos and walks; the trees and flowers
vary every day, the sight of all in general presenting
delights to their minds, whilst the varieties in particular, continually renew those delights ; and
whereas they correspond to things divine, and the
inhabitants are in the science of correspondences,
they are always filled with new knowledges, and
by those new knowledges their spiritual-rational
principle is perfected : these are their delights, because gardens, beds of flowers, grass-plots, and trees,
correspond to sciences, to knowledges, and thence
to intelligence. They, again, who have ascribed
all things to the Divine Being or Principle, and
have regarded nature respectively as dead, only sub-

servient to things spiritual, and have confirmed
themselves in such belief, are in heavenly light;
so that all things which appear before their eyes,
derive from that light a transparency, in which
they behold innumerable variegations of light,
which variegations their internal sight, as it were,
immediately imbibes, whence they perceive interior delights : the things which appear in their
houses are, as it were, adamantine, in which are
similar variegations. I have been told, that the
walls of their houses are, as it were, chrystaline, thus
also transparent, and in them appear as it were
floating forms, representative of things celestial,
and this also with perfect variety : these effects re- .
sult from the circumstance, that such transparency
corresponds to an intellect enlightened by the Lord,
the shadows being removed which arise from the
faith and love of natural objects. Such are the
things, and infinite others, concerning which it is
said by those who have been in heaven, that they
have seen what eye hath never seen, and, from the
perception of divine things communicated to them
from those things, that they have heard what the
ear hath never heard.

They, again, who have not dealt clandestinely,
but have been desirous that all things which they
thought should be exposed to view, so far as was
consistent with civil life, inasmuch as they thought
nothing but what was sincere and just from the
Divine Being, have lucid faces in heaven, and in

their faces, by virtue of that lucidity, singular their
affections and thoughts appear as in a form, and as
to their speech and actions, they are as it were
the effigies of their affections; hence they are loved
more than others: when they speak, the face con-
tracts a degree of obscurity; but when they have
done speaking, the same things which they spoke,
appear together in the face fully exposed to view:
all things likewise which exist around them, inasmuch as they correspond to their interiors, are
in such an appearance, that it is perceived clearly
by others what they represent and signify: the
spirits who have had delight in clandestine deal-
ings, when they see them at a distance, shun them,
and appear to themselves to creep away from them
like serpents.

They, again, who have regarded adulteries as
enormous, and have lived in the chaste love of marriage, are above all others in the order and form of
heaven, and hence in all beauty, and continually in
the flower of youth; the delights of their love are
ineffable, and they increase to eternity; for into
that love all the delights and joys of heaven flow,
because that love descends from the conjunction of
the Lord with heaven, and with the church, and in
general from the conjunction of good and truth,
which conjunction is heaven itself in general, and
with every individual angel in particular: their
external delights are such as cannot be described
by human expressions. But these are only a few

of the things which have been told me concerning the correspondences of delights with those who are principled in heavenly love.

From what hath been said, it may be known, that the delights of all after death are turned into correspondent ones, the love itself still remaining to eternity, as conjugial love, the love of what is just, sincere, good, and true; the love of sciences and of knowledges, the love of intelligence and wisdom, and all other loves : the things which thence flow, as streams from their fountain, are delights which likewise remain, but are exalted to a higher degree when raised from natural delights to spiritual.

Self-Examination.

" What is my real love ?
On what is fix'd my mind ?
Are my affections rais'd above,
Or downward all inclin'd ?

" Important question this,
On which alone depend
My future states of woe or bliss,
When this short life shall end !

" If worldly, vain desire,
And carnal motives reign,
My portion is infernal fire
And never-ending pain.

" If heav'nly and divine
All my affections be,
The holy, happy state is mine,
Through all eternity."

SECTION III.

SHEWING that no one cometh into Heaven, from immediate Mercy.

" Who will render to every man according to his deeds : tribulation and anguish, upon every soul of man that doeth evil ; but glory, honour, and peace, to every man that worketh good ; to the Jew first, and also to the Gentile : for there is no respect of persons with God." ROM. ii. 6, 9, 10, 11.

AN opinion hath prevailed with some, that God turns away His face from man, rejects him from Himself, and casts him into hell, and that He is angry with him on account of evil; and with some it is supposed still further, that God punisheth man, and doth evil to him.   In this opinion they confirm themselves from the literal sense of the Word, where expressions to that effect occur, not being aware that the spiritual sense of the Word, which explains the literal sense, is altogether otherwise; and that hence the genuine doctrine of the church, which is from the spiritual sense of the Word, teacheth otherwise, viz. that the Lord never turns away His face from man, and rejects him from Himself; that He doth not cast any one into hell, and that He is not angry with any one. Every one also whose mind is in a state of illustration, when he reads the Word, perceives this to be the case, from this consideration alone, that God is Good itself, Love itself, and Mercy itself; and that Good itself cannot do evil to any one; also that Love itself, and Mercy itself cannot reject man from itself, because it is contrary to the very essence of Mercy and Love, thus contrary to to the Divine Principle itself; wherefore, they who think from an enlightened mind, when they read the Word, clearly perceive, that God never turns Himself away from man; and since He never turns Himself away from man, that He deals with him from a principle of Good, of Love, and of Mercy ; that is, that He willeth his good, that He loveth him, and that He is merciful to him. Hence also they see, that the literal sense of the Word in which such things are said, conceals in itself a spiritual sense, according to which those expressions are to be explained, which, in the sense of the letter, are spoken in accommodation to the apprehension of man, and according to his first and common ideas.

Evil spirits are severely punished in the world of spirits, that by punishments they may be deterred from doing evil : This likewise appears as if it were from the Lord, when yet there is nothing of punishment in that world, from the Lord, but from evil itself: for evil is so conjoined with its own punishment, that they cannot be separated; for the infer-

nal crew desire and love nothing more than to do
evil, especially to inflict punishment, and to torment;
and they likewise do evil, and inflict punishment on
every one who is not protected by the Lord; wherefore, when evil is done from an evil heart, in such
case, since it rejects from itself all protection from
the Lord, infernal spirits rush in upon him who
doeth such evil, and punish him. This may in
some measure be illustrated by the case of evils and
their punishishments in the world, where also they
are conjoined; for laws in the world prescribe punishment for every evil; wherefore he who rushes
into evil, rushes also into the punishment of evil;
the only difference is, that evil may be concealed in
the world, but not in the other life. From these
considerations it may be manifest, that the Lord
doeth evil to no one, and that the case in this respect is like as in the world, where neither a king,
nor a judge, nor the law, is the cause of punishment
to a guilty person, because they are not the causes
of evil with the evildoer.

They who are not instructed concerning heaven,
and concerning the way to heaven, also concerning the life of heaven appertaining to man, again suppose, that to be received into heaven is the mere effect
of mercy, which is granted to those who are in faith,
and for whom the Lord intercedes,—thus that it is
merely admission out of favour; consequently that all
men whatsoever may be saved by virtue of the Lord's
good pleasure; yea, some conceive that this may be

the case even with all in hell. But such persons are totally unacquainted with the nature of man, not being aware that his quality is altogether such as his life is, and that his life is such as his love is, not only as to the interiors, which are of his will and understanding, but as to the exteriors, which are of his body, and that the corporeal form is only an external form, in which the interiors present themselves in effect, and hence that the whole man is his love, as above shown in Part II. of Section I. Nor are they aware, that the body doth not live from itself, but from its spirit, and that the spirit of man is his very affection itself, and that his spiritual body is nothing else but the man's affection in a human form, in which also it appears after death. So long as these particulars are unknown, man may be induced to believe, that salvation is nothing but the good pleasure of the Lord, which is called mercy, and grace or favour.

But it may be expedient first to say what divine mercy is. Divine mercy is pure mercy towards the whole human race, for the purpose of saving them; and it is likewise continual with every man, and in no case recedes from any one, so that every one is saved who can be saved: but no one can be saved but by divine means, which means are revealed by the Lord in the Word. Divine means are what are called divine truths; these teach in what manner man ought to live, that he may be saved; by those truths the Lord leads man to heaven, and by them implants in man the life of heaven; this the Lord effects with all; but the life of heaven cannot be implanted in any one, unless he abstains from evil, for evil opposes; so far, therefore, as man abstains from evil, so far the Lord leads him, out of pure mercy, by His divine means, and this from infancy to the end of his life in the world, and afterwards to eternity : this is the divine mercy which is meant. Hence it is evident, that the mercy of the Lord is pure mercy, but not immediate, that is, such as to save all out of good pleasure, let them live as they may.

The Lord never acts contrary to order, because He Himself is Order. The divine truth proceeding from the Lord is what makes order, and divine truths are the laws of order, according to which the Lord leads man; wherefore to save man by immediate mercy is contrary to divine order, and what is contrary to divine order, is contrary to the Divine Being or Principle. Divine order is heaven appertaining to man, which order man had perverted with himself, by a life contrary to the laws of order, which are divine truths; into that order man is brought back by the Lord, out of pure mercy,* by

---

* A very prevailing idea is, that DIVINE MERCY if carried beyond a certain limit, would clash or interfere with DIVINE JUSTICE, according to the well known saying—" A God all mercy is a God unjust;" but which unjust idea is entirely owing to our making a distinction between those divine attributes, when

means of the laws of order: and so far as he is brought back, so far he receives heaven in himself, and he who receives heaven in himself, comes into

---

in reality none exists; for if properly considered it will be found that with the Lord, MERCY and JUSTICE are only different names for one and the same thing, agreeably to what is written—" *Unto Thee, O Lord, belongeth* MERCY; *for Thou* RENDEREST TO EVERY MAN ACCORDING TO HIS WORK," Psalm lxii. 12.: where we find that it is MERCY in the Lord to act with JUSTICE, or to render to every man according to his work. Nor is it different as to the mercy which a king exercises towards a criminal, by remitting or commuting his punishment; for in such case the king assumes the character of the judge, and acts accordingly, thus with justice.

It is evidently in consequence of making a distinction between those two divine attributes, that the prevailing misconception as to the doctrine of ATONEMENT, has arisen: for it is generally supposed, that the Lord came into the world to make atonement or satisfaction to the *vindictive justice* (as it is called) of God the Father; and that in consequence thereof, God the Father was disposed, for His sake, to forgive the sins of mankind, and thus again to receive them into favour! But the truth is, that God the Father (who is the Lord God the Saviour Himself,) had no *vindictive justice* to satisfy, but was solely prompted, from pure love and mercy, and consequently justice, to become the REDEEMER as well as the CREATOR of the world, agreeably to what is written, " IN HIS LOVE AND IN HIS PITY, HE REDEEMED THEM," Isa. lxiii. 9.; "THOU, O JEHOVAH, ART OUR FATHER, OUR REDEEMER," verse 16.; " LOOK UNTO ME, AND BE YE SAVED, ALL THE ENDS OF THE EARTH: FOR I AM GOD, AND THERE IS NONE ELSE." Isa. xlv. 22.; besides many other places to the same effect, shewing clearly that JEHOVAH HIMSELF is our Redeemer and Saviour, and *none else.* But admitting for a moment, that Jesus was a separate Being or Per-

heaven.   Hence it is again evident, that the divine
mercy of the Lord is pure mercy, but not immediate
mercy.   If men could be saved by immediate mercy,

son from the Father, and that the latter, before He could pardon
or remit the sins of mankind, required that His justice should be
satisfied by the vicarious sufferings and death of the Son, is it
not obvious that this would be an act of the greatest *injustice*,
to require that the innocent should suffer in the room of
the guilty?   Besides, as it is allowed that the Son was God
equally with the Father, and that consequently, the sins of
mankind were committed equally against *Him*, how comes it
that *His* justice did not require to be satisfied as well as the
Father's, before *He* could forgive them?   There is no allusion
to any thing of the kind in what the Lord said to him who en-
quired what he must do to inherit eternal life [Mark x. 17.];
nor in that touching parable of the returning prodigal [Luke xv.];
which parable we are authorised to consider as an exact description of the fallen state of man, and also of the means of his reconciliation, or acceptance with God.

If, therefore, the Lord God the Creator, in becoming our Redeemer, had only His own pure love and mercy to satisfy, and
nothing whatever of *justice*, at least in the sense in which it is
commonly understood; and if, as we have seen above, there
are not *two* divine persons—the one a God *all mercy*, and
the other a God *all justice*, it is very evident that the prevailing
idea on the subject of ATONEMENT, which is solely founded
thereon, must fall to the ground, being so obviously at variance
both with the Sacred Scriptures and the plain dictates of
reason.   The true idea on the subject is, that at the time of
our Lord's coming, mankind had so estranged themselves from
God, or, what amounts to the same, the power of hell
had so far prevailed over the power of heaven, (in the
minds of men,) that the whole human race were in dan-
ger of perishing, being without the power of " working out

all would be saved, even they who are in hell, yea, neither would there be a hell, because the Lord is Mercy Itself, Love Itself, and Good Itself; where-

---

their own salvation," or becoming regenerate; and therefore, had the Lord not come at the time He did, and rescued the human race from this deplorable state, " no flesh could have been saved." But, for ever adored be the Divine Mercy! the Lord, "in the fulness of time," did come, "travelling in the greatness of His strength," and fought, and overcame, and rescued the prey, as it were, out of the lion's mouth; or in other words, the Lord by the divine process which He underwent while in the flesh, so subdued the power of hell or the devil, (for He says, " Now is the prince of this world cast out," John xii. 31.; see also Luke x. 18.) that the minds of men were delivered from the state of thraldom in which the prince of this world at that time held them, and were restored to such a state of spiritual liberty, as by the use of the appointed means they might become regenerate, and thus be restored to that state of integrity from which they had fallen, or in which man originally stood before the fall.   This, then, is the proper idea which ought to be entertained on the subject of ATONEMENT, to which it is evident we are solely indebted for the power or liberty which we now possess of working out our own salvation.

Hence we see it depends wholly on man himself whether this ATONEMENT, which the Lord, of His divine mercy, effected, will be of any avail to him, as it depends wholly on the use which he makes of the appointed means, his *receiving the atonement,* or becoming *reconciled to God ;* for whether we speak of *reconciliation* or *at-one-ment,* it means the same thing, as the same word, the learned say, literally stands for both in the original language. "At present the word *atonement* occurs only once in the New Testament: that is in Rom. v. 11., where the Apostle says, And not only so, but we also joy in God through our Lord Jesus Christ, by whom we have received the *atonement.*' It is

fore it is contrary to His Divine Principle to say,
that He is able to save all immediately, and doth
not save them : it is a thing known from the Word,

---

not a little extraordinary, that a word which occurs but once in
the whole of the New Testament, from which more especially
Christians profess to derive their creed, should have come to
occupy so great a space in the language of the theology of the
day. And it is more extraordinary still, that it should have
come to be supposed that the Lord made an atonement *to the
Father*, thus that the atonement was *received by the Father*
when yet it is said, in the only text of the New Testament
where the word occurs, that it is *WE who have received the
atonement.* The reason is, because the proper meaning of the
word has been little attended to ; which is, as stated above,
reconciliation. This was the only meaning which the word bore
when the Scriptures were translated ; although, like the words
person, ghost, and others, it has since assumed a different signification ; and men have been too much influenced in their religious sentiments, by the changes which have gradually taken
place in the meaning of words. In every other place, the
same word, and its corresponding verb, are translated *reconciliation,* and *to reconcile.* Thus in the verses preceding that just
quoted from Romans, our translators say, ' For if, when we
were enemies, we were *reconciled* to God by the death of His
Son, much more, being *reconciled,* we shall be saved by His
life :' then follows, ' And not only so, but we also joy in God
through our Lord Jesus Christ, by whom we have received the
atonement.' Here then *atonement* is used as the answering sub-
stantive to the verb *to reconcile.* *Atonement,* is literally *at-one-
ment ;* the state of being *at one,* or, *in agreement.* See Acts
vii. 26. 1 Macc. xiii. 50. 2 Macc. i. 5. ; vii. 33. Though the
word *atonement* occurs but once in the New Testament, it is
often used in the Old, but always in the sense of *reconciliation.*

that the Lord willeth the salvation of all, and the damnation of no one.

The generality of those who come from the chris-tian world into the other life, bring along with them the above faith, that they are to be saved by immediate mercy, for they implore that mercy; but on examination it is found that they believed, that to come into heaven consists in mere admission, and that they who are let in, enter into heavenly joys, being not at all aware of what heaven is, and of what heavenly joy is; wherefore they are told, that heaven is not denied by the Lord to any one, and that they may be let in if they desire it, and may likewise tarry there; on which occasion they who desire it are also admitted, but when they are at the very threshold, they are seized with such torture of the heart from the breathing of heavenly heat, which is the love wherein the angels are principled, and from the influx of heavenly light, which is di-vine truth, that they apperceive in themselves infer-nal torment, instead of heavenly joy, and in conse-quence of the shock they throw themselves head-long thence : thus they are instructed by living ex-perience, that heaven cannot be given to any one from immediate mercy.

Doubtless, then, the atonement of Christian doctrine is *recon-ciliation with God*, including the means by which reconciliation is effected." See " AN APPEAL IN BEHALF OF THE VIEWS," &c.

I have occasionally discoursed on this subject
with the angels, and have told them that the generality of those in the world who live in evils, when
they discourse with others concerning heaven, and
concerning eternal life, express no other idea than
that to come into heaven consists merely in admission from mere mercy, and that this belief is
principally maintained by those who make faith
the only medium of salvation; for such persons,
from their principles of religion, have no respect to
the life, and to the deeds of love which make life,
thus neither to any other means by which the Lord
implants heaven in man, and renders him receptible of heavenly joys; and whereas they thus reject
every actual means, they establish the necessary con-
sequences, flowing from their own persuasions, that
man comes into heaven from mercy alone, to which
they believe that God the Father is moved by the
intercession of the Son. To these observations the
angels replied, that they were aware that such a
tenet follows of necessity from the preconceived
principle respecting faith alone, and, inasmuch as
that tenet is the head of all the rest, and, since it
is not true, is not admissive of any light from heaven, that hence comes the ignorance which prevails
in the church at this day, concerning the Lord,
concerning heaven, concerning the life after death,
concerning heavenly joy, concerning the essence of
love, and charity, and in general concerning good,
and concerning its conjunction with truth, conse-

quently concerning the life of man, whence it is
and what is its quality, which yet no one ever derives from thought, but from will, and consequent
deeds, and only so far from thought, as the thought
is grounded in the will, thus not from faith, only
so far as faith is grounded in love.

The angels grieve at the thought, that these same
persons are not aware that faith alone cannot
exist with any one, inasmuch as faith without its
origin, which is love, is merely science, and with
some a kind of persuasion which has the semblance
of faith, which persuasion is not in the life of man,
but out of it, for it is separated from the man if it
doth not cohere with his love. They further said,
that they who are confirmed in such a principle
concerning the essential medium of salvation appertaining to man, cannot do otherwise than believe in
immediate mercy, because they perceive from natural lumen, and likewise from the experience of
sight, that faith separate doth not make the life of
man, since they who lead an evil life can think and
persuade themselves of doctrinal truths, in like manner with those who lead a good life: hence it comes
to be believed, that the wicked can be saved alike
with the good, provided only that at the hour of
death they speak with confidence concerning intercession, and concerning the mercy which it pro-
cures.

The angels professed, that as yet they have never
seen any one, who had lived an evil life, received

M

into heaven by immediate mercy, howsoever he
might have spoken in the world from that trust or
confidence, which, in an eminent sense, is understood by faith.   On being questioned concerning
Abraham, Isaac, Jacob, and David, and concerning
the Apostles, whether they were not received into
heaven of immediate mercy, they replied, not one of
them ; and that every one was received according
to his life in the world ; and that they knew where
they were ; and that they are not in more estimation there than others.   The reason, they said,
why such honourable mention is made of them in
the Word, is because by them, in the internal sense,
is meant the Lord : by Abraham, Isaac, and Jacob,
the Lord, as to His Divine Principle, and the Divine Human ; by David, the Lord as to the Regal Divine Principle ; and by the Apostles, the Lord as to
divine truths ; and that they have no apperception
of them whatsoever, whilst the Word is read by
man, inasmuch as their names do not enter heaven,
but instead of them, they have a perception of the
Lord, as was just now observed ; and that therefore,
in the Word, which is in heaven,* they are no where
mentioned, inasmuch as that Word is the internal
sense of the Word which is in the world.

I can testify, from much experience, that it is impossible to implant the life of heaven in those who

---

* That the WORD is in heaven, see Psalm cxix. 89. Rev. xiv. 6.

have led lives in the world opposite to the life of
heaven : for there were some who believed that they
should easily receive divine truths after death, when
they heard them from the angels, and that they
should give credit to them, and hence should live
otherwise than they had done, and thus that they
might be received into heaven : but trial was made
in many instances, yet only with those who were
in such belief, to whom the trial was permitted for
the purpose of convincing them that no repentance
is given after death : some of them with whom the
trial was made, understood truths, and seemed to
receive them, but instantly on turning to the life
of their love, they rejected them, yea, argued a-
gainst them : some rejected them immediately, being unwilling to hear them : some were desirous
that the life of love which they had contracted
from the world, might be taken away from them,
and that angelic life, or the life of heaven, might
be infused in its place ; this likewise, by permis-
sion, was accomplished ; but when the life of their
love was taken away, they lay as dead, and had no
longer the use of their faculties.

From these and other cases of experience, the
simply good were instructed, that the life of any
one cannot in any wise be changed after death,
and that evil life cannot any how be transmuted
into good life, or infernal life into angelic, inasmuch as every spirit, from head to foot, hath a
quality agreeable to his love, and consequently a

quality agreeable to his life, and that to transmute
this life into the opposite, is altogether to destroy
the spirit.   The angels declare, that it is easier to
change a bat into a dove, and an owl into a bird of
paradise, than an infernal spirit into an angel.

From these considerations, it may now be manifest, that no one can be received into heaven by
immediate mercy.

Reconciliation ;

or

Acceptance with God.

" As we our sins remove,
And put them far away,
Return to God in humble love,
And His commands obey ;
So shall we be forgiv'n,
And conscious peace receive,
Witness with joy an inward heav'n,
And on the Lord believe.

" As evils are abhor'd,
In heart, in life, and mind ;
They are remitted by the Lord,
And we forgiveness find :
O let us then remove
All evil from the heart ;
That JESUS may His truth and love,
With heav'nly peace, impart !"

SECTION IV.

SHEWING that it is not so difficult as it is supposed, to live a Life which leads to Heaven.

" Whosoever will come after Me, let him deny himself, and take up his cross, and follow Me.'—MARK viii. 34.

SOME people believe, that to lead a life which leads to heaven, which is called spiritual life, is difficult, by reason they have been told, that man must renounce the world, and deprive himself of the concupiscences which are called the concupiscences of the body and of the flesh, and that he must live a spiritual life; which things they conceive as implying, that they must reject worldly things, which consist chiefly in riches and honours, that they must walk continually in pious meditation about God, about salvation, and about eternal life, and that they must spend their life in prayer, and in reading the Word and other pious books; this they call renouncing the world, and living in the spirit and not in the flesh: but that the case is altogether otherwise, hath been given me to know from much experience, and from conversation with the angels,

M 2

yea, that they who renounce the world and live in
in the spirit in the manner above described, procure to themselves a sorrowful life, which is not receptible of heavenly joy, for every one's life remains with him after death; but to the intent that
man may receive the life, of heaven, it is altogether
necessary that he live in the world, and in office
and employment there, and that in such case by
moral and civil life he receive spiritual, and that
spiritual life cannot otherwise be formed with man,
or his spirit prepared for heaven; for to live internal life, and not external at the same time, is like
dwelling in a house which hath no foundation,
which successively either sinks into the ground, or
becomes full of chinks and breaches, or totters till it
falls down.

If the life of man be viewed and explored by
rational intuition, it is discovered to be threefold,
viz. spiritual life, moral life, and civil life, and that
those lives are distinct from each other; for there
are men who live a civil life, and yet not a moral
and spiritual life; and there are men who live a moral life, and still not a spiritual; and there are
those who live both a civil life, a moral life, and a
spiritual one together; the latter are they who live
the life of heaven, but the former are they who
live the life of the world separate from the life of
heaven. From these considerations it may be manifest, in the first place, that spiritual life is not

separate from natural life, or from the life of the world, but that the former is conjoined with the latter as the soul with its body, and that if it were separated, it would be like dwelling in a house which had no foundation, as was said above. For natural and civil life is the activity of spiritual life, since spiritual life consisteth in willing well, and moral and civil life in acting well; and if the latter be separated from the former, spiritual life consisteth merely in thought and speech, and will recedes, because it hath no support; nevertheless will is the very spiritual principle itself of man.

That it is not so difficult as is generally supposed, to live a life that leads to heaven, may be seen from what now follows. Who cannot live a civil and moral life, since every one from infancy is initiated into it, and, from life in the world, is acquainted with it? Every one also brings it into act, the bad and the good alike; for who is not willing to be called sincere, and who is not willing to be called just? Almost all exercise sincerity and justice in externals, insomuch that they appear as if they were sincere and just in heart, or as if they acted from sincerity itself and justice: the spiritual man ought to live in like manner, which he may do as easily as the natural man, but with this difference only, that the spiritual man believes in a Divine Being or Principle, and that he acts sincerely and justly, not merely because it is agreeable to civil and moral laws to do so, but also because it is a-

greeable to divine laws; for the spiritual man, inasmuch as his thoughts, when he acts, are occupied
by divine things, communicates with the angels of
heaven, and so far as this is the case, so far he is conjoined with them, and thus his internal man is opened,
which, viewed in itself, is a spiritual man: when man
is of such a character and quality, he is then adopted
and led by the Lord, whilst he himself is not aware of
it, and in such case the acts of sincerity and justice,
which relate to moral and civil life, are performed by
him from a spiritual origin; and to perform acts of
sincerity and justice from a spiritual origin, is
to perform them from the very principle itself of
sincerity and justice, or to perform them from the
heart. His justice and sincerity, in the external
form, appears altogether like the justice and sincerity appertaining to natural men, yea, appertaining
to evil men and infernals, but in the internal form
they are altogether dissimilar: for evil men act justly and sincerely, merely for the sake of themselves
and the world; wherefore unless they feared the law
and its penalties, also the loss of reputation, of honour, of gain, and of life, they would act altogether
insincerely and unjustly, inasmuch as they neither
fear God nor any divine law, thus neither are they
restrained by any internal bond; wherefore to the ut-
most of their power, in such case, they would defraud, plunder, and spoil others, and this from delight: that they are inwardly of such a character,
appears principally from persons of a similar character in the other life, where external things are re-

moved from every one, and his internals are opened, in which finally they live to eternity; for all such, inasmuch as they then act without being restrained by external bonds, which, as was said above, are the fear of the law, of the loss of reputation, of honour, of gain, and of life, act insanely, and laugh at sincerity and justice. But they who have acted sincerely and justly under the influence of divine laws, when external things are taken away, and they are left to things internal, act wisely, because they are conjoined with the angels of heaven, from which wisdom is communicated to them. From these considerations it may now first be manifest, that the spiritual man can act altogether in like manner as the natural man, as to civil and moral life, provided he be conjoined to the Divine Being or Principle as to the internal man, or as to will and thought, as already shewn.

The laws of spiritual life, the laws of civil life, and the laws of moral life, are also delivered in the TEN PRE-CEPTS OF THE DECALOGUE: in the three first, the laws of spiritual life; in the following four, the laws of civil life; and in the three last, the laws of moral life :*

---

* It is here to be noted, that the Author adopts the division of the commandments as it is received in the Swedish Church ; agreeably to which division, the *first* commandment includes both the *first* and *second*, according to the division in the Church of England; thus the *three first* commandments in the Swedish division, includes the *four first* of the English division, whilst the *last* in the English division is divided into *two* in the Swedish division.

the merely natural man lives, in the external form, according to the same precepts, in like manner as the spiritual, man for in like manner he worships the Divine Being, frequents the temple, hears sermons, composes his face to devotion, doth not commit murder, nor adultery, nor theft, doth not bear false witness, doth not defraud his companions of their goods; but these things he doth merely for the sake of himself and the world, to keep up appearances; hence the same person, in the internal form, is altogether opposite to what he appears in the external, because in heart he denies the Divine Being, in worship plays the hypocrite, when left to himself and his own thoughts, he laughs at the holy things of the church, believing that they serve merely as a bond to bind the simple vulgar : hence it is, that he is altogether disjoined from heaven, consequently, not being a spiritual man, he is neither a moral man nor a civil man ; for although he doth not commit murder, still he bears hatred towards every one who opposes him, and in consequence of hatred burns with revenge; wherefore, unless civil laws, and external bonds, which are fears, restrained him, he would commit murder ; and since this is his governing desire, it follows, that he is continually committing murder : again, although he doth not commit adultery, he is perpetually an adulterer, because he is in the commission of adultery, so far as ability and licence are given : a person of the same description, although he doth not steal, yet, inasmuch as he covets the

goods of others, and regards fraud and evil artifices
as no offences against jurisprudence, in mind he is
continually playing the part of a thief: the case
is similar as to the precepts of moral life, which
teach not to bear false witness, and not to covet
the goods of others.   Such is the character of every
man who denies the Divine Being or Principle,
and who hath not a conscience grounded in religion; that such is his proper character, appears
manifestly from similar spirits in the other life,
when, on the removal of things external, they are
let into their internals, on which occasion, inasmuch
as they are separated from heaven, they act in unity
with hell, wherefore they are consociated with those
who are in hell.

It is otherwise with those who have in heart
acknowledged the Divine Being, and in the tran-
sactions of their lives have had respect to divine
laws, and have acted according to the three first
precepts of the decalogue equally as according to
the rest: when these, on the removal of things external, are let into their internals, they become
wiser than when in the world; for when they come
into their internals, it is like coming from shade into light, from ignorance into wisdom, and from a
sorrowful life into a blessed one, inasmuch as they
are in the Divine Being or Principle, thus in heaven.   These observations are made to the intent
that both the quality of the one and the quality of

the other may be known, although both have lived a similar external life.

Every one may know that thoughts are conveyed and tend according to intentions, or in the direction which a man intends; for thought is the internal sight of man, which in this respect is like the external sight, that it is turned in the direction, and there abides, in which it is bent and intended: if, therefore, the internal sight or thought be turned to the world, and there abides, it follows that the thought becomes worldly; if it be turned to self and self-honour, it follows that it becomes corporeal; but if it be turned to heaven, it follows that it becomes heavenly; consequently, if it be turned to heaven, that it is elevated; if to self, that it is drawn down from heaven, and immersed in what is corporeal; and if to the world, that it is also bent down from heaven, and diffused amongst those objects which are presented to the eyes. It is the man's love which makes his intention, and which determines his internal sight or thought to its objects; thus the love of self to itself and its objects, the love of the world to worldly objects, and the love of heaven to heavenly objects; from which considerations it may be known what is the quality of the state of man's interiors, which are of his mind, provided his love be known, viz. that the interiors of him who loves heaven are elevated towards heaven, and are open above; and that the interiors of him who loves the world, and who loves himself,

are closed upwards, and are open exteriorly: hence
it may be concluded, that if the superior principles
of the mind are closed upwards, man can no longer
see the objects which are of heaven and the church,
and that those objects are in thick darkness in respect to him, and the things which are in thick darkness are either denied or not understood: hence it
is that they who love themselves and the world
above all things, inasmuch as the superior principles
of their minds are closed, in heart deny divine
truths, and if they discourse at all about them from
memory, still they do not understand them; they
regard them also in the same manner that they regard worldly and corporeal things; and since they
are of such a character, they cannot pay attention
to any thing but what enters through the senses of
the body, with which also they are alone delighted;
thus they are delighted with many things so entering, which are likewise filthy, obscene, profane, and
wicked, which things cannot be removed, because
with such persons there is no influx given from
heaven into their minds, inasmuch as these are
closed above, as was before observed. The intention
of man, from which his internal sight or thought is
determined, is his will; for what a man wills, this he
intends, and what he intends this he thinks; wherefore if his intention be towards heaven, his thought
is determined thither, and with it his whole mind,
which is thus in heaven, whence he looks down-
wards upon the things of this world which are be-

neath him, as a person looking from the roof of a
house; hence it is that the man who hath the interiors of his mind open, can see the evils and falses which appertain to him, for these are beneath
the spiritual mind; and on the other hand, that the
man whose interiors are not open, cannot see his
own evils and falses, because he is in them, and not
above them: from these considerations a conclusion
may be formed respecting the origin of wisdom in
man, and the origin of insanity, also what will be
the quality of man after death, when he is left to
will and to think, likewise to act and to speak, according to his interiors. These observations are
also made with a view to its being known what is
the quality of man interiorly, howsoever he appears
exteriorly like to another.

That it is not so difficult to live the life of heaven as is believed, is evident now from this consideration, that nothing more is necessary than for man
to think, when any thing presents itself to him
which he knows to be insincere and unjust, and to
which he is inclined, that it ought not to be done,
because it is contrary to the divine preeepts; if he
accustoms himself so to think, and from so accus-
toming himself, acquires a habit, he then by degrees
is conjoined to heaven; and so far as he is conjoined to heaven, so far the higher principles of his
mind are opened, and so far as those principles are
opened, so far he sees what is insincere and unjust;
and in proportion as he sees these evils, in the same

proportion they are capable of being shaken off, for it is impossible that any evil can be shaken off until it be seen: this is a state into which man may enter from a free principle; for who is not capable of thinking as above, from a principle of freedom? But when he has made a beginning, then the Lord operates all sorts of good with him, and gives him the faculty not only of seeing evils, but also of not willing them, and finally of holding them in aversion: this is meant by the Lord's words, "*My yoke is easy, and My burden light,*" Matt. xi. 30. It is however to be noted, that the difficulty of so thinking, and likewise of resisting evils, increases in proportion as man committeth evil from the will; for in the ssme proportion he accustoms himself to evils, until at length he doth not see them; and is next led to love them, and from the delight of love to excuse them, and by all kinds of fallacies to confirm them, saying that they are allowable and good; but this is the case with those who, in in the age of adolescence, plunge into evils as without restraint, and then at the same time reject divine things from the heart.

In respect to the Lord's words at the head of this section, by *cross* are meant temptations, and by *following the Lord* is meant to acknowledge His Divinity, and to do His precepts: the reason why temptations are meant by a *cross* is, because evils, and the false principles thence derived, which adhere to man from his birth, infest and thus torment those who are natural, during the time that they be-

come spiritual; and whereas evils and the false
principles thence derived, which infest and torment,
cannot be dispered but by temptations, hence temptations are signified by a *cross ;* on this account the
Lord saith, that his followers are to *deny themselves,
and take up their cross,* that is, that they are to reject whatever is of self, their *cross* being the self-
hood of man, against which they are to engage in
combats; so in another place, " Jesus said to the
rich man who asked him what he ought to do, that
he might inherit eternal life, Thou knowest the commandments, thou shalt not commit adultery, thou
shalt not kill, thou shalt not steal, thou shalt not bear
false witness, thou shalt not defraud, honour thy
father and thy mother : he answering, said, All these
have I kept from my youth. Jesus looked at him, and
loved him; yet He said unto him, One thing thou lackest, go thy way, sell what thou hast, and give to the
poor, so shalt thou have treasure in the heavens; and
come, take up the cross, and follow Me," Mark, x.
17, 19, 20, 21.; here also by *following the Lord, and
taking up the cross,* similar things are signified as
above, viz. to acknowledge the Divinity of the
Lord, and the Lord to be the God of heaven
and earth, for without that acknowledgment, no
one can abstain from evils, and do good, except
from himself, and except it be meritorious. The
good, which is truly good, and not meritorious,
is only from the Lord, wherefore unless the Lord
be acknowledged, and that all good is from Him,

man cannot be saved ; but before any one can do
good from the Lord, he must undergo temptation;
the reason is, because by temptation the internal of
man is opened, by which man is conjoined to heaven. Now since no one can do the precepts without the Lord, therefore the Lord said, *yet lackest thou
one thing, sell all that thou hast, and follow Me, taking up the cross*, that is, that he ought to acknowledge the Lord, and undergo temptations. That he
should SELL ALL THAT HE HAD, *and give to the poor,*
in the spiritual sense signifies, that he should alien-
ate and reject from himself the things of self; thus
it signifies the same as above, that *he should deny
himself.* And by *giving to the poor*, in the spiritual
sense, is sginified, the doing works of charity; the
reason why the Lord so spake to the rich man was,
because he was rich ; and by *riches*, in the spiritual
sense, are signified the knowledges of what is good
and true; hence it may be manifest, that the Lord
spake here, as in other places by correspondences.

That *to go after the Lord*, and to *follow Him*,
is to deny self, is evident ; and to *deny self*, is not
to be led of self, but of the Lord ; and he denies
himself who shuns and holds in a aversion all evils,
because they are sins, which when man holds
in aversion, he is led of the Lord, for he doeth
His precepts not from himself, but from the Lord.
Similar things are signified in other passages also
by following the Lord, as Matt. xix. 21, 28.; Mark
ii. 14, 15.; iii. 7, 8.; x. 21, 28, 29.; Luke xviii.

N 2

22, 28.; John xii. 26. : xiii. 36, 37.; xxi. 19—22.
From these considerations it may be manifest, that
to *follow the Lord* is to be led by Him, and not
by self; and no other person can be led by the Lord,
except him who is not led by himself; and every
one is led by himself, who doth not shun evils, because they are contrary to the Word, and thus are
contrary to God, consequently because they are
sins from hell; every one who doth not thus shun
evils, and hold them in aversion, is led by himself;
the reason is, because the evil which is hereditarily
in man, makes his life, inasmuch as it is his self-
hood, and man, before those evils are removed, doeth
all things from them, thus from himself. But it is
otherwise when evils are removed, as is the case
when they are shunned, because they are infernal;
for in this case the Lord enters with truths and
goods out of heaven, and leads man : the primary
cause is, because every man is his own love, and
man, as to his spirit, which lives after death, is nothing but the affection which is of his love, and
every evil is from his love, thus it is of his love;
hence it follows, that the love or affection of man
cannot otherwise be reformed, but by the shunning
of evils and holding them in spiritual aversion,
which is to shun and hold them in aversion, because
they are infernal. From these considerations, it
may now be manifest what it is to follow the
Lord.

It hath been granted me to discourse with some

in the other life who had removed themselves
from worldly business, that they might live piously
and holily, and likewise with some who had afflict-
themselves by various methods, because they believed that this was to renounce the world, and to
subdue the concupiscences of the flesh ; but most of
them, inasmuch as they had thence contracted a sorrowful life, and had removed themselves from the life
of charity, which life can only be led in the world,
cannot be consociated with the angels, because the life
of the angels is a life of gladness, resulting from bliss,
and consists in performing acts of goodness, which
are works of charity: and besides, they who have
led a life abstracted from worldly engagements, are
heated with the idea of their own merits, and hence
are continually desirous of heaven, and continually
thinking of heavenly joy, as a reward, being altogether ignorant of what constitutes heavenly joy ; and
when they are introduced amongst angels, and into
their joy, which is without merit, and consists in
exercises and manifest offices, and in the blessedness
resulting from the good which they thereby pro-
mote, they are surprised, like persons who discover
something quite foreign to their belief; and whereas
they are not receptible of that joy, they depart, and
consociate with spirits of their own way of thinking,
who had lived a similar life in the world. But they
who have lived holily in externals, being continually
in places of worship, and engaged in acts of prayer, and
who have afflicted their souls, and at the same time

have continually cherished an idea respecting themselves, that they would thus be esteemed and honoured above others, and at length after death be
accounted saints, in the other life are not in heaven, because they have done such things for the
sake of themselves; and whereas they have defiled
divine truths by the self-love in which they have
immersed them, some of them are so insane as to
think themselves gods, wherefore they are in hell a-
mongst those of a like description.

These observations are made to the intent that it
may be known, that the life which leads to heaven
is not a life abstracted from the world, but in the
world; and that a life of piety without a life of charity, which is only given in the world, doth not lead
to heaven; but that a life of charity which consists
in acting sincerely and justly in every function, in
every engagement, and in every work, from an interior principle, thus from a celestial origin, (which
origin is in that life when man acts sincerely and
justly because it is agreeable to the divine law,)
doth lead to heaven: this latter life is not difficult,
but a life of piety abstracted from a life of charity
is difficult, which life nevertheless leads away from
heaven, in the same proportion that it is believed to
lead to heaven.

ON THE

SECOND ADVENT;

OR,

NEW CHRISTIAN CHURCH.

" And I John saw the Holy City, NEW JERUSALEM, coming down from God out of heaven, prepared as a Bride adorned for her Husband. And I heard a great voice out of heaven, saying, Behold the tabernacle of GOD is with men, and He will dwell with them, and they shall be His people, and GOD Himself shall be with them their God. And GOD shall wipe away all tears from their eyes; and there shall be no more death, neither sorrow, nor crying, neither shall there be any more pain, for the former things are passed away." Rev. xxi. 2, 3, 4.

THE reason why a New Church is meant by the New Jerusalem coming down from God out of heaven, Rev. xxi. is, because Jerusalem was the metropolis of the land of Canaan; there were the temple and the altar, and there also sacrifices were offered, and there consequently divine worship itself was performed, which every male throughout the whole land was required to attend three times a-year: A further reason is, because the Lord was in Jerusa lem, and taught in its temple, and afterwards glorified His Humanity there: this then is the true ground why the church is signified by Jerusalem. That the church is meant by Jerusalem, appears clearly from the prophetical parts of the Old Testament, where, speaking of the New Church which was to be instituted by the Lord, it is there called Jerusalem. I shall adduce the following passages only, from which any one endued with interior reason may see, that by Jerusalem is meant the church: "Behold, I create a NEW HEAVEN AND A NEW EARTH, and the former shall not be remembered nor come into mind; behold, I CREATE JERUSALEM for an exultation, and her people for gladness, and I will exult over JERUSALEM, and be glad over My people. Then the wolf and the lamb shall feed together; they shall not hurt nor destroy in all the mountain of My holiness," Isaiah lxv. 17, 19, 25. "Awake, awake, put on thy strength, O Zion; put on the garments of thy beauty, O JERUSALEM, the city of holiness; for henceforth there shall no more come into thee the uncircumcised and the unclean; shake thyself from the dust, arise, and sit down, O JERUSALEM: My people shall know My name; they shall know in that day that I am He that doth speak, Behold, It is I: Jehovah hath comforted His people, He hath redeemed JERUSALEM," chap. lii. 1, 2, 6, 9. "Sing, O daughter of Zion, be glad with all thy heart, O daughter of JERUSALEM; the king of Israel is in the midst of thee; fear not evil any more; He will be glad over thee with joy; He will rest in thy love; He will exult over thee with sing-

ing; I will give you for a name and a praise among
all people of the earth," Zeph. iii. 14—17, 20. That
the church which was to be instituted by the Lord,
is meant by Jerusalem in these passages, and not
the city of Jerusalem inhabited by the Jews, is
plain from every particular of its description; as that
Jehovah God would create a new heaven and a new
earth, and also Jerusalem at the same time; and
that this Jerusalem would be a crown of glory, and
a royal diadem; that it was to be called holiness,
and the city of truth, the throne of Jehovah, a quiet
habitation, a tabernacle that should not be taken
down; that the wolf and the lamb should feed together there, that the mountains should drop new
wine, and the hills flow with milk, and that it should
remain from generation to generation; beside other
circumstances, as respecting the people there, that
they should be holy, all written for life, and should
be called the redeemed of Jehovah.

Moreover, all those passages relate to the coming
of the Lord, particularly to His second coming, when
Jerusalem shall be such as it is there described; for
before this she was not married; that is, made the
Bride and the Wife of the Lamb, as the New Jerusalem is declared to be in the Revelation. The former or present church is meant by *Jerusalem* in
Daniel; and its commencement is described by these
words: "Know therefore and understand, that from
the going forth of the Word to the restoration
and the building of JERUSALEM, even unto Messiah
the Prince, shall be seven weeks; and after three-

score and two weeks the streets shall be built again,
and the trenches, but in troublesome times," chap. ix.
25.; its end, however, is described in these words :
"At length upon the bird of abomination shallbe desolation, and even to the consummation and decision
it shall drop on the devastation," verse 27.; this end
is described by these words of the Lord in Matthew :
" When ye shall see the abomination of desolation
spoken of by Daniel the prophet standing in the
holy place, let him that readeth understand," chap.
xxiv. 15.   That Jerusalem, in the passages above
adduced, does not mean the city of Jerusalem, which
was inhabited by the Jews, may appear from many
places in the Word, as where it is said of that city
that it was entirely destroyed, and that it was to
be pulled down, as Jer. v. 1.; vi. 6, 7.; vii. 17, 18.;
viii. 6, 7, 8.; ix. 10, 11, 12.; xiii. 9, 10, 14.; xiv. 16,
Lam. i. 8, 9, 17. Ezek. iv. 1. to the end; chap. v. 9.
to the end, chap. xii. 18, 19.; xv. 6, 7, 8.; xvi. 1—63.
xxiii. 1—40. Matt. xxiii. 37, 38. Luke xix. 41—44.
xxi. 20, 21, 22.; xxiii. 28, 29, 30.; besides many
other passages; and also where it is called Sodom,
Isa. iii. 9. Jer. xxiii. 14. Ezek. xvi. 46, 48, and in
other places.

That since the creation there have been four
churches in general on this earth, in a regular succession one after another, may appear both from
the historical and the prophetical parts of the Word,
but especially from the book of Daniel, where those
four churches are described by the statue that ap-

peared to Nebuchadnezzar in a dream, chap. ii. and
afterwards by the four beasts ascending out of the
sea, chap. vii. The first church, which may be
called *the Most Ancient*, was extant before the flood,
and its consummation or end is described by the
flood. The second church, which may be called
the Ancient, was in Asia, and part of Africa, and
this was brought to its consummation and destruction by idolatries. The third church, which was
the Israelitish, began at the promulgation of the
decalogue on Mount Sinai, was continued by the
Word written by Moses and the prophets, and was
consummated or ended by its profanation of the
Word, which profanation was at its fulness when
the Lord came into the world; wherefore, He being
the Word, they crucified Him. The fourth church,
is *the Christian*, which the Lord established by the
evangelists and the apostles; this church has had
two epochs, one extending from the time of the
Lord till the council of Nice, and the other from
that council to the present time; this latter, however, in its progress, was divided into three branches, the Greek, the Roman-Catholic, and the Reformed; nevertheless all these three are called Christian. Moreover, within every general church there
have been several particular churches, which, notwithstanding their separation from the general, have
still retained its name, as is the case with the different heresies in the Christian church.

That the last time of the Christian church is the

very night in which former churches have set, is plain from the Lord's prediction concerning this night in the evangelists and in Daniel; in the evangelists, from these circumstances, "That they should see the abomination, and that there should be great affliction, such as was not from the beginning of the world, neither shall be; and that unless those days should be shortened no flesh could be saved;" and lastly, "that the sun shall be darkened, the moon shall not give her light, and the stars shall fall from heaven," Matt. xxiv. 15, 21, 22, 29. In other passages in the evangelists, that time is also called night; as in Luke: "In that night there shall be two in one bed, the one shall be taken and the other shall be left," chap. xvii. 34.; and in John, "I must work the works of Him that sent Me, while it is day; the night cometh when no man can work," chap. ix. 4. Since all light departs at midnight, and the Lord is the True Light, John i. 4.; viii. 12, xii. 35, 36, 46.; therefore He said to His disciples, when He ascended into heaven, "Lo! I am with you alway, even unto the consummation of the age,"* Matt. xxviii. 20.; and then He departs from them to a new church.

---

* In the common English version of the Bible, instead of THE CONSUMMATION OF THE AGE, this passage is translated, THE END OF THE WORLD; it will, however, be admitted by every one who is acquainted with the original, that the former is the true signification.

That this last time of the church is the very night in which former churches have set, is plain also from this passage in Daniel: " In the end, upon the bird of abominations, shall be desolation, even until the consummation and decision, it shall drop upon the devastation,"* chap. ix. 27.: that this prophecy relates to the end of the Christian church, is very plain from the Lord's own words, Matt. xxiv. 18.; the same too is evident from this passage in Daniel relating to the fourth kingdom, or the fourth church, represented by the image which Nebuchadnezzar saw : " And whereas thou sawest iron mixed with miry clay, they shall mingle themselves with the seed of man, but they shall not cleave one to another, even as iron is not mixed with clay," chap. ii. 43: the seed of man is the truth of the Word.   It is further evident from this passage relative to the fourth church represented by the fourth beast ascending out of the sea : " I saw in the night visions, and behold, a fourth beast, terrible and dreadful, it shall devour the whole earth, and tread it down, and break it in pieces," chap. vii. 7, 23.; which expressions mean, that every truth of the church should be brought to a consummation, and then there will be night, because the truth of

---

* In the common translation, these words are rendered, *a consumption, even determined;* whereby the distinction is lost between *consummation* and *decision;* but the original Hebrew favours the construction here given by our author.

the church is light. Many similar things are predicted of this church in the Revelation, especially
in the sixteenth chapter, where it speaks of the
vials of the anger of God poured out upon the earth,
signifying the falsities which should then overflow
and destroy the church. There are also several
passages in the prophets to the same purpose; as for
example, " Shall not the day of Jehovah be darkness and not light, even very dark, and no brightness in it?" Amos v. 20, Zeph. i. 15.; and again,
" In that day, if one look unto the land, behold
darkness and sorrow, and the light is darkened in
the ruins thereof," Isa v. 30.; viii. 22.: the day of
Jehovah is the day of the Lord's advent.

The Lord is present with every man, and is ur-
gent and instant to be received (see Rev. iii. 20.),
and when man receives Him, which he does by ac-
knowledging Him to be his God, his Creator, Redeemer, and Saviour, it is then His first advent,
which is called day-dawn: from this period, man, as
to his understanding, begins to be enlightened in
spiritual subjects, and to advance towards a wisdom
more and more interior; and as he receives such
wisdom from the Lord, such in proportion is his
progression from morning to mid-day; and this
mid-day continues with him to old age, even till
death, and after death he is elevated into heaven to
the Lord Himself, where, though he may have died
an old man, he is restored to the morning of his

life, and continues to eternity to grow in that wisdom which was implanted in the natural world.

It is the prevailing opinion at this day, in every church, that the Lord, when He comes to the last judgment, will appear in the clouds of heaven, with angels, and the sound of trumpets; that He will gather together all who are then dwelling on the earth, as well as all who are deceased, and will separate the evil from the good, as a shepherd separates the goats from the sheep; that then He will cast the evil, or the goats, into hell; and raise up the good, or the sheep, into heaven: and further, that He will at the same time create a new visible heaven, and a new habitable earth, and on the latter He will cause a city to descend, which is to be called the New Jerusalem, and is to be built, according to the description given in the Revelation (chap. xxi.), of jasper and gold, and the foundation of its walls of every precious stone, and its height, breadth, and length, equal, each twelve thousand furlongs; and that all the elect are to be gathered together into this city, both those that are then alive, and those that have died since the beginning of the world; and that the latter will then return into their bodies and enjoy everlasting bliss in that magnificent city, as in their heaven. This is the prevailing opinion of the present day, in all christian churches, on the coming of the Lord and the last judgment.

In regard to the state of souls after death, both universally and particularly, it is the common belief at this day, that human souls, after death, are mere aerial beings, of which it is impossible to form any idea but as of a vapour or exhalation; and that such being their state and nature, they are reserved to the day of the last judgment, either in the middle of the earth, where their *Pu* is placed, or in the *limbus* of the ancient Fathers:* But on these points there are various opinions; some suppose them to be ethereal or aerial forms, and thus that they are like ghosts and spectres, certain of them dwelling in the air, others in the woods, and others in the waters; some again suppose that the souls of the deceased are translated to the planets or to the stars, and there have their abodes allotted them; and some again, that, after thousands of years, they return back into material bodies; but the general supposition is that they are reserved till the time when the whole firmament, together with the terraqueous globe, will be destroyed, and that this is to be effected by fire, either bursting from the centre of the earth,

---

* Did we not meet with such extravagant notions as these, maintained and propagated every day in the writings of some modern philosophers, we might be inclined to suspect the truth of this assertion, from an idea of the impossibility of the human mind ever suffering itself to be blinded by such grovelling and ill-grounded conceits, instructed as it might be by the light of Divine Revelation. How much is it to be lamented, that such wretched sophistry should ever pass in the world under the sacred and venerable name of philosophy!

or cast down from heaven in a universal blaze of
lightning; that then the graves will be opened,
and the souls that were reserved, will be clothed
again with their bodies, and be translated into that
holy city, Jerusalem, there to dwell together on
another earth, in purified bodies, some in a lower
region, some in a higher, for the height of the city
will be twelve thousand furlongs, the same as its
length and its breadth, Rev. xxi. 16.

When a clergyman or layman is asked whether he
firmly believes all these things, as that the antidelu-
vians, along with Adam and Eve, and the postdelu-
vians, with Noah and his sons, and also that Abraham, Isaac, and Jacob, with all the prophets and apostles, are, in like manner as the souls of all other
men, still reserved in the middle of the earth, or
flying about in the æther, or air; and also whether
he believes that their souls will be again clothed
with their bodies, and again enter into connexion
with carcases eaten by worms, by mice, by fish, or,
as in the case of Egyptian mummies, by men, and
with skeletons parched in the sun, and reduced to
powder; and further, whether he believes that the
stars of heaven will fall upon the earth, which
yet is smaller than any of them;—if clergymen or
laymen, I say, be asked whether they believe all
this, or whether such conceits are not mere para-
doxes, which, like all other contradictory notions,
are dispelled and dissipated by right reason, some
of them will make no reply; some will insist that

such points are matters of faith, to which the understanding must be kept in obedience; some again will agree, that not only these things, but also many others, which are above the comprehension of reason, are works of divine omnipotence; and when they mention faith and Omnipotence, sound reason is banished, and either disappears like a thing annihilated, or becomes like a spectre, and is called insanity: to this they will add, "Are not such opinions agreeable to the Word? and ought not that to be the rule and measure of our thoughts and speech?"

That the Word, as to the letter, is written by appearances and correspondences, and that thus there is a spiritual sense contained in each expression, in which sense truth appears in its light, whilst the sense of the letter is in shade, has been already shewn. Lest, therefore, the members of the New Church should wander, like those of the Old, in the shade of the literal sense of the Word, particularly on the subjects of heaven and hell, and of a life after death, and on this of the coming of the Lord, it has pleased the Lord to open the sight of my spirit, and thus to let me into the spiritual world, permitting me not only to converse with spirits and angels, and with my relations and friends, nay, with kings and princes, who have departed out of the natural world, but also to behold the stupendous sights of heaven, and the miserable scenes of hell, demonstrating by this, that man does

not live after death in any region of the earth called *Pu* or *limbus,* nor flit about blind and dumb
in air, or emptiness, but that he lives a man in a
substantial body, and in a far more perfect state, if
he goes amongst the blessed, than when he lived
before, in a material body.

To prevent man from plunging deeper into this
false opinion of the destruction of the visible heaven and the habitable earth, and thereby of the
spiritual world, in consequence of that ignorance
which has given rise to so much naturalism and
atheism; and to prevent such naturalism and atheism from spreading as a mortification in a limb,
through man's external mind, whence his speech
originates, in a like manner as they have already
begun to affect and take root in the interior rational
mind, especially among the learned, I have been en-
joined by the Lord, to publish some of the various
circumstances of what I have seen and heard, as
well concerning HEAVEN AND HELL, as the LAST
JUDGMENT; and also to unfold the APOCALYPSE,
, which treats of the Lord's coming, of the former
heaven, of the new heaven, and of the Holy Jerusalem; which, when read and understood, will enable
every one to see what is there meant by the coming
of the Lord, by the new heaven, and by the New
Jerusalem.

That the coming of the Lord is to form a new
heaven of those who have believed on Him, and to
establish a new church of those who shall hereaf-

ter believe on Him, is grounded in this circumstance, that these two purposes are the end of His
coming. That it is not to destroy any thing, but
to build up, consequently not to condemn, but
to save those who have believed on Him since
His first coming, and who shall hereafter believe
on Him, is plain from these words of the Lord:
" God sent not His Son into the world to condemn
the world, but that the world through Him might
be saved; he that believeth on Him is not condemned, but he that believeth not is condemned already,
because he hath not believed in the name of the
only begotten Son of God," John iii. 17.; and in
another place, " If any man hear My words and
believe not, I judge him not, for I came not to
judge the world, but to save the world: he that
rejecteth Me, and receiveth not My words, hath one
that judgeth him; the Word that I have spoken,
the same shall judge him," chap. xii. 47, 48.   The
very end of the creation of the universe was solely
this, that an angelic heaven might be formed out of
mankind, where all who believe in God, might live
in eternal blessedness; for the divine love which is
in God, and which essentially is God, can intend
nothing else; and the divine wisdom, which is also
in God, and is God, can produce nothing else.
Since, then, the creation of the universe had for its
end an angelic heaven, to be formed out of the human
race, and at the same time a church on earth, man's
passage into heaven lying through the church; and

since the salvation of mankind, being effected upon men that are born in the world, is thus a continuation of creation, therefore we so frequently meet in the Word with the term *to create*, the meaning of which is to form for heaven; as in the following passages: " CREATE in me a clean heart, O God, and renew a right spirit within me," Ps. li. 10.: " Thou openest Thy hand, they are filled with good, Thou sendest forth Thy spirit, they are CREATED," Ps. civ. 28, 30.: " The people which shall be CREATED shall praise the Lord," Ps. cii. 18.: " Thus saith Jehovah that CREATED thee, O Jacob, and He that FORMED thee, O Israel : I have redeemed thee, I have called thee by My name; every one that is called by My name, I have CREATED him for My glory," Isa. xliii. 1, 7.: " They were prepared in thee in the day that thou wast CREATED; thou wast perfect in thy ways from the day that thou wast CREATED, till iniquity was found in thee," Ezek. xxviii. 13, 15.; this is spoken of the king of Tyre: " That they may see and know, and consider, and understand together, that the hand of Jehovah hath done this, and the Holy One of Israel hath CREATED it," Isa. xli. 20. Hence the meaning of *creating* in the following passages will appear : " Thus saith Jehovah, He that CREATETH the heavens, He that spreadeth forth the earth, He that giveth breath unto the people upon it, and spirit to them that walk therein," Isa. xliii. 5. ; xlv. 12, 18. : " Behold, I CREATE A NEW HEAVEN AND A NEW EARTH :

Be glad and rejoice for ever in that which I CRE-
ATE; for behold, I CREAT JERUSALEM a rejoicing,"
Isa. lxv. 17, 18.

It is written in many places, that the Lord will
come in the clouds of heaven, as Matt. xvii. 5.;
xxiv. 30.; xxvi. 64. Mark xiv. 61, 62. Luke ix.
34, 35.; xxi. 27. Rev. i. 7.; xiv. 14. Dan. vii. 13.
But no one hath heretofore known what is meant
by the clouds of heaven, and hence mankind have
believed that the Lord will appear in them in person. Thus it has remained undiscovered to this day,
that the Word, in its literal sense, is meant by the
clouds of heaven, and that the spiritual sense of the
Word is meant by the power and glory in which also
the Lord is to come, Matt. xxiv. 30.; for no one until
this time has had the least conjecture of there being
in the Word any spiritual sense, such as it is in reality
and truth. Now, whereas the spiritual sense of the
Word has been opened to me by the Lord, and it
has been granted me to be with the angels and spirits in their world as one of themselves; it has been
revealed to me, that by the clouds of heaven, the
Word, in its natural sense, is meant, and by glory,
the Word in its spiritual sense, and by power, the
effectual operation of the Lord by the Word. That
the clouds of heaven have this signification, may be
seen from the following passages in the Word:
" There is none like unto the God of Jeshurun, who
rideth in the heaven, and in his magnificence in the
CLOUDS," Deut. xxxiii. 26. " Sing unto God; sing

praises to His name; extol Him that rideth upon
the CLOUDS," Psalm lxviii. 4. "Behold, the Lord
rideth upon a SWIFT CLOUD," Isaiah xix. 1.: To
ride, signifies to instruct in divine truths from the
Word; for a horse signifies the understanding of
the Word, as may be seen in the APOCALYPSE RE-
VEALED, n. 298.: for who cannot see that God does
not ride on the clouds? Again, "God rode upon the
cherubs, His pavilion round about Him were thick
CLOUDS OF THE HEAVENS," Psalm xviii. 10—13.: cherubs also signify the Word, as may be seen in the same
work, n. 239, 672. "Jehovah bindeth up the waters in His thick CLOUDS; He spreadeth His CLOUD
upon His throne," Job xxvi. 8, 9.: "Ascribe ye
strength unto Jehovah, His strength is in the
CLOUDS," Psalm lxviii. 34.: "Jehovah hath created
upon every dwelling place of Mount Zion a CLOUD by
day, and upon all the glory shall be a COVERING,"
Isaiah iv. 5. The Word, in its literal sense, was
also represented by the cloud in which Jehovah descended on Mount Sinai, when He delivered the
law; the precepts of the law which were at that time
delivered, being the first fruits of the Word.

In confirmation of what hath been said, the following particulars may be mentioned: There are
clouds in the spiritual world, just as in the natural
world, but from another origin; in the spiritual
world there are sometimes bright clouds above the
angelic heavens, but over the hells hang dusky
clouds; the bright clouds over the angelic heavens

P

are a representative of obscurity there, proceeding from the literal sense of the Word; but the dispersion of those clouds signifies, that they are then in clearness from its spiritual sense; but the dusky clouds over the hells, signify the falsification and profanation of the Word. The origin of this signification of clouds in the spiritual world, is grounded in this circumstance, that the light which proceedeth from the Lord as a sun there, signifies divine truth, whence He is called the Light, John i. 9. chap. xii. 35.; it is on this account too that the Word itself, which in that world is kept deposited in the sacred recesses of their temples, appears encompassed with a bright light, and the light is obscured by the interposition of clouds.

That the Lord is the Word, is evident from this passage in John: " In the beginning was the Word, and the Word was with God, and the Word was God; and the Word was made flesh," chap. i. 1, 14.; that the Word in this passage is divine truth, is plain from this consideration, that christians obtain divine truth from no other source than the Word, which is a fountain from which all churches that take their name from Christ, draw living waters in their fulness; and yet, in the natural sense of the Word, divine truth is in a cloud; but in its spiritual and celestial sense, it is in glory and in power. That there are three senses in the Word, the natural the spiritual and the celestial, one within the other, is shewn in the work ON THE SACRED SCRIPTURES:

Hence it appears, that the Word mentioned in John, signifies divine truth. John also testifieth the same in his first epistle: "We know that the Son of God is come, and hath given us an understanding, that we may know the TRUTH, and we are in the TRUTH, in His Son JESUS CHRIST. This is the True God and Eternal Life," chap. v. 20. It is for this reason that the Lord so often said, " VERILY, I say unto you," for AMEN (which is the word translated VERILY), in the Hebrew tongue, is TRUTH: and for the same reason He is called the AMEN, Rev. iii. 14.; and the TRUTH, John xiv. 6. If you consult also the learned, what they understand by the Word spoken of in John i. 1. they will tell you, they understand the Word in its supereminence; and what else is the Word in its supereminence, but divine truth? From these considerations it is evident, that the Lord will now also appear in the Word; the reason why He will not appear in person, is because, since His ascension into heaven, He is in His glorified Humanity, and in that Humanity He cannot appear to any man, unless the eyes of his spirit be first opened; and this opening cannot be effected in any that are in evils, and the falses thence derived,—thus not in any of the goats whom He setteth on His left hand; wherefore when He shewed Himself to His disciples, He first opened their eyes, for it is written, "And their eyes were opened, and they knew Him, and He vanished out of their sight," Luke xxiv. 31. The case was the same with the women who visited the sepulchre, and His conversing with them, whom yet it is impossible for any man to see with the material eye. It is plain from His transfiguration before Peter, James, and John, that the apostles, before the Lord's resurrection, did not see Him in His glorified Humanity, with their bodily eyes, but in the spirit, (which vision appeareth after waking as if it was seen in sleep,) for it is written, " *their eyes were heavy with sleep,*" Luke ix. 32. It is then a vain thing to imagine, that the Lord will appear in the clouds of heaven in person, when the truth is, that He will appear in the Word, which is from Him, and is thus Himself.*

---

* The carnal mind, we are well aware, will make many objections to this idea of the Lord's Second Advent, and will think the glory of that advent hereby much diminished and degraded. But let it be remembered, that the carnal or natural man always sees the things of God through a false medium, and therefore cannot possibly be a competent judge of what is, or is not, agreeable to the divine glory. Thus the Jews of old deceived themselves with false notions concerning the glory of their expected Messiah, under His first advent; they looked for a great prince, or deliverer, who should appear amongst them in the outward pomp and parade of a mighty conqueror, to rescue them from their temporal enemies; and few, very few, had their eyes enlightened by the purities of heavenly light, to discern the glories of the Messiah, in the low sphere in which He appeared, and see the lustre of His advent, in opening and establishing a spiritual kingdom of heavenly righteousness and truth in the hearts of His people,

Since the Lord, therefore, cannot manifest Himself in person [to the world], which has just been shewn to be impossible, and yet He has foretold, that He would come and establish a New Church, which is the New Jerusalem, it follows, that He will effect this by the instrumentality of a man, who is able not only to receive the doctrinals of that church in his understanding, but also to make them known by the press. That the Lord manifested Himself before me, His servant, that He sent me on this office, and afterwards opened the sight of my spirit, and so let me into the spiritual world, permitting me to see the heavens and the hells, and also to converse

through the light and power of His divine Word. The case most probably will be the same at this day; the carnal christian, looking for Christ's coming in great outward pomp, in the clouds of the external heavens, to reign visibly and in person on earth, will be offended to hear of His coming only in the spiritual sense of His Word, which is divine good and divine truth, to establish His spiritual kingdom in the hearts of His people, and will possibly think this a lessening and diminution of the lustre of His advent. But the truly spiritual Christian will be enlightened and delighted to see, that herein the glory of the Lord is truly revealed, and that no advent could possibly be more glorious than this appearing of the great Jehovah Jesus in the spiritual sense of that Holy Word, which is Himself, and from Him, and full of Him, and effective of conjunction with Him, in all such as truly receive that Word into their hearts, and let it operate in their lives and conversation.—May every reader, for his own sake, take this subject into deep and serious consideration.

with angels and spirits, and this now continually for many years, I attest in truth : and further, that from the first day of my call to this office, I have never received any thing appertaining to the doctrines of that church from any angel, but from the Lord alone, *whilst I was reading the* WORD.

The presence of the Lord is continual with every one, whether he be wicked or good, for without His presence no man can live; but His coming is with those only who receive Him, and these are they who believe on Him, and do His commandments. The continual presence of the Lord is the efficient cause of man's rationality, and of his capacity to become spiritual; this is an effect of the light that proceeds from the Lord, as the sun in the spiritual world, which light man receives with his understanding; and this light is truth, by which he enjoys rationality; but the coming of the Lord is with such as conjoin heat with that light, that is, with such as conjoin love with truth; for the heat proceeding from the same sun is love to God and towards our neighbour. The mere presence of the Lord, and the illustration of the understanding thereby, may be compared with the presence of solar light in the natural world, which, unless it be conjoined with heat, cannot prevent a universal desolation on the face of the earth. But the coming of the Lord may be compared with the coming of heat, as in the time of spring, in consequence of which, and its conjunction with light, the earth is softened, and the seeds sown therein begin to vegetate, and bear fruit: such a parallelism is there between spiritual things, with which the spirit of man is connected, and natural things, with which his body is connected.

That the Church is at an end when there is no longer any faith within the Church, is known from the Word; but it is not as yet known that there is no faith where there is no charity; wherefore something shall now be said relative to this subject. That there would be no faith at the end of the Church, is foretold by the Lord, in these words: "When the Son of Man shall come, will He find FAITH on the earth?" Luke xviii. 8. And also that then there would be no charity, is foretold in these, "In the consummation of the age, iniquity shall be multiplied; the CHARITY of many shall grow cold; and this Gospel shall be preached to all the world; and then shall the end come," Matt. xxiv. 12. The consummation of the age is the last time of the Church: the successive states of the declension of the Church, with respect to love and faith, are described by the Lord in that chapter: but they are described by mere correspondences; and therefore the things which are there predicted by the Lord, cannot be understood, unless the spiritual sense corresponding with every particular, be known, agreeably to the explanation which is given of that chapter in the work entitled, ARCANA CÆLESTIA. Such then is the state of the Church at this day, that there is no faith therein, because there is no charity; and where there is no charity, there is nothing of spiritual good, for that good is solely derived from charity or neighbourly love, originating in the acknowledgment and love of the Lord, as the only God of heaven and earth.

That the Christian Church, such as it is at this day, is consummated and laid waste to so great an extent, as that there is not a single genuine truth at this time remaining in it; and also, that unless a New Church were to be raised up in place of the present, " *no flesh could be saved*," cannot be seen by those who have confirmed themselves in its falses, because a confirmation of the false, is a denial of the true; and for this reason, he who is in such a state, places, as it were, a vail beneath his understanding, and so keeps guard, that nothing else creeps in to pull down the ropes and stakes by which he has built up and put together his theological system, like a strong tent.   Add to this, that the natural-rational principle can confirm whatsoever it pleases, whether it be false or true, and both, when confirmed, appear in similar light; nor is it known whether the light be false, such as is experienced in a dream, or whether it be true, such as is seen in the clear day: but the case is altogether otherwise with the spiritual-rational principle, such as they enjoy who look to the Lord, and from Him are in the love of truth.   Hence it is, that every church composed of such as see by the above light of confirmation, appears to itself as if it were the only church which enjoyed the light of truth, whilst all others which differ from it, are in darkness; for they who see by the light of confirmation, are not unlike owls, which see light during the shades of night, but in the day time see the sun and its rays as thick darkness. Such was, and such also is, every church which is in falses, when once it is founded by leaders, who being sharp-sighted as lynxes in their own conceit, form to themselves a morning light from their own understandings, and an evening light from the Word. For, did not the Jewish Church, when it was altogether laid waste, which was the case when our Lord came into the world, contend loudly, by its scribes and lawyers, that because it possessed the Word, it was the only church which was in heavenly light, although at that very time they crucified the Messiah or Christ, who was the Word Itself, and the All in All thereof? And what does the church, which in the prophets and the Revelation is understood by Babylon, contend for else, but that she is the queen and mother of all churches, and that others, which recede from her, are illegitimate children, who ought to be excommunicated; and this notwithstanding she has thrust down the Lord the Saviour from His throne and altar, and placed herself thereon in his stead? Does not every church, be it ever so heretical, when once it is established, fill all countries and cities with a cry that it is the only one which is orthodox, and æcumenical, and that it is in possession of the Gospel,

which the flying angel preached in the midst of
heaven? Rev. xiv. 6. And who does not hear the
voice of the vulgar, echoing the same cry? Who can
speak with stronger persuasion of the certainty of
his phantastic opinions, than an atheistical natural-
ist? and how heartily does he laugh at the divine
operations of God, the celestial principles of heaven,
and the spiritual principles of the church! What
lunatic does not fancy his own infatuation to be
wisdom, and another's wisdom to be infatuation?
Not to mention other cases of a similar kind. These
instances are adduced for the sake of illustration,
and to evince that it cannot be discovered by natural light alone, before truth shineth in its own light
from heaven, that the church is come to its consummation, in other words, that it is in mere falses; for
the false does not see the true, but the true sees the
false; and every man is so constituted, that he can
see and comprehend the truth, when he hears it;
but if he is confirmed in falses, he cannot introduce
it into his understanding, so as that it may remain
there, because he can find no place for it; and if
by chance it gain admission, the crowd of falsities
before collected, cast it out as heterogeneous.

It has been already shewn, that there have been,
from the beginning, in common, four churches on
this earth; one before the flood, another after the
flood, a third called the Israelitish Church, and a
fourth the Christian; and as all churches depend on
the knowledge and acknowledgement of one God,

with whom the members of the church can have conjunction, and none of the four churches above named, have been in that truth, it follows, that a church is to succeed those four, which shall know and acknowledge the one God; for the divine love of God could have had no other end or design in creating the world, but to conjoin man to Himself, and Himself to man, and thus to dwell with him.

That the former churches were not in the truth, is plain from this circumstance, that the Most Ancient Church, which existed before the flood, worshipped the invisible God, with whom there can be no conjunction; so likewise did the Ancient Church, which existed after the flood; the Israelitish Church worshipped Jehovah, who in Himself is the invisible God, Exod. xxxiii. 18—23., but under a human form, which Jehovah God put on by means of an angel, and in which form He was seen by Abraham, Sarah, Moses, Hagar, Gideon, Joshua, and sometimes by the prophets, which human form was representative of the Lord who was to come, and thus being representative, therefore all and every thing in that church were made representative also: indeed it is well known that their sacrifices and other ceremonies of worship, were representative of the Lord who was to come, and that they were abrogated at His coming. But the fourth church, which was called Christian, did indeed acknowledge one God with the lips, but in three persons, each whereof singly or by himself was God, and thus acknowledged a divided trinity, and not united in one Person, the consequence of which was, that an idea of three gods was fixed in the mind, notwithstanding the declaration of the lips in favour of one; and moreover, the doctors of the church insist from that very doctrine of theirs, which they composed after the council of Nice, that men ought to believe in God the Father, God the Son, and God the Holy Ghost, all three invisible, because existing in a like divine essence before the world was; when yet, as was said above, there can be no conjunction with an invisible God; for they are not yet aware that the one God, who is invisible, came into the world, and assumed the Humanity, not only that He might redeem man, but also that He might be made visible, and thus such as they might have conjunction with, for it is written, " The Word was with God, and THE WORD WAS GOD, AND THE WORD WAS MADE FLESH," John i. 1, 14.; and in Isaiah, " Unto us a child is born, unto us a son is given, and His name shall be called, the MIGHTY GOD, THE EVERLASTING FATHER," chap. ix. 5.; and in the prophets it is frequently declared, that Jehovah Himself would come into the world, and be the Redeemer, which was also done in the Humanity which He assumed.

The reason why this New Church is the crown of all the churches which have been to this time on the terrestrial globe, is, because it will worship one Visible God, in whom is the Invisible God, as the soul is in the body; for thus, and no otherwise, can conjunction be effected between God and man; the reason of which is, because man is natural, and consequently thinks naturally, and the conjunction must be effected in his thought, and so in the affection of his love, and such conjunction is produced when man thinks of God as a Man. Conjunction with an invisible God is like the conjunction of ocular sight with the expanse of the universe, of which it sees no end; it is also like sight in the midst of the ocean, which falls on air and water, and is lost in their immensity; but conjunction with a visible God, is like the visible appearance of a man in the air or on the sea, stretching forth his hands, and inviting to his embraces: for all conjunction of God with man must be likewise reciprocal on the part of man with God, and this reciprocality on man's part is not possible but with a visible God. That God was not visible before He assumed the Humanity, the Lord Himself teacheth in John: " Ye have neither heard the voice of the Father, nor seen His shape," chap. v. 37.; and in Moses, "That no man can see God and live," Exod. xxxiii. 20: but that He is seen by His Humanity is declared in John: " No one hath seen God at any time; the only begotten Son, who is in the bosom of the Father, He hath brought Him forth to view," chap. i. 18.; and again, " Jesus said, I am the Way, the Truth, and the Life, no one cometh to the Father but by Me; he that knoweth Me knoweth the Father, and he that seeth Me seeth

Q

the Father," chap. xiv. 6, 7, 9. That conjunction is effected with the invisible God, by Him who is visible, that is, by the Lord, He Himself teaches in these words, " Abide in Me, and I in you; he that abideth in Me, and I in him, the same bringeth forth much fruit," John xv. 4, 5, " In that day ye shall know that I am in the Father, and ye in Me, and I in you," chap. xiv. 20. " The glory which Thou gavest Me, I have given them, that they may be one, even as We are one; I in them, and thou in Me, that the love wherewith thou hast loved Me, may be in them, and I in them," chap. xvii. 21, 22, 23, 26.; and chap. vi. 56. Also that the Father and He are one; and that it is necessary to believe on Him, to attain eternal life. That salvation dependeth on conjunction with God, has been abundantly shewn above.

That this church is to succeed the churches which have been extant from the beginning of the world, and that it will endure for ages of ages, and is thus to be the crown of all churches that have been before it, was foretold by the prophet Daniel, first when he related and explained to Nebuchadnezzar his dream concerning the four kingdoms, by which the four churches, represented by the statue that appeared to him, are understood; for he says, " In the days of these kings shall the God of heaven set up a kingdom which shall never be destroyed, and it shall consume all these kingdoms, but it shall stand for ever," chap. ii. 44.; and that this should be effected by a "stone that became a great rock, and filled the whole earth," verse 35.: By a rock, in the Word, the Lord is meant, as to divine truth. The same prophet says in another place, " I saw in the night visions, and behold, one like the Son of Man came with the clouds of heaven, and to Him was given dominion, and glory, and a kingdom, that all people, nations, and languages should serve Him: His dominion is an everlasting dominion, which shall not pass away, and His kingdom that which shall not be destroyed," chap. vii. 13, 14.; and this he says after he had seen the four beasts ascending out of the sea, verse 3. by which also the four former churches were represented: That this prophecy of Daniel hath relation to the present time, is evident from his words, chap. xii. 4.; and also from the Lord's words, Matt. xxiv. 15, 30. The like is said in the Revelation, " And the seventh angel sounded, and there were great voices in heaven, saying, The kingdoms of this world are become the kingdoms of our Lord, and of His Christ, and He shall reign for ever and ever," chap. xi. 15.

But beside these, the other prophets have in many passages foretold this church, and its future state: from which it may suffice to adduce these few : It is written in Zechariah, " There shall be one day, which shall be known to Jehovah, not day nor night, because about evening time there shall be light; and in that day living waters shall go out from Jerusalem, and Jehovah shall be King over all the earth;

in that day shall there be one Jehovah, and His name
One," chap. xiv. 7, 8, 9.: in Joel, " It shall come to
pass in that day, that the mountains shall drop new
wine, and the hills shall flow with milk, and Jerusalem shall remain to generations of generations," chap. iii. 18, 20.: in Jeremiah, "At that
time they shall call Jerusalem the throne of Jehovah, and all nations shall be gathered, because of
the name of Jehovah, to Jerusalem, neither shall
they walk any more after the confirmation of
their evil heart," chap. iii. 17. Rev. xxi. 24, 26.:
in Isaiah, " Thine eyes shall see Jerusalem a quiet
habitation, a tabernacle that shall not be taken
down; not one of the stakes thereof shall ever
be removed, neither shall any of the cords thereof be broken," chap. xxxiii. 20.: in these passages the holy New Jerusalem is meant, which is
described in the Revelation, chap. xxi. and by this
again, the New Church.   Again, in Isaiah, " There
shall come forth a Rod from the stem of Jesse, and
righteousness shall be the girdle of his loins, and
truth the girdle of his thighs; the wolf shall also
dwell with the lamb, and the leopard shall lie
down with the kid, and the calf and the young
lion, and the fatling together, and a little child
shall lead them; and the cow and the bear shall
feed, their young ones shall lie down together;
and a sucking child shall play on the hole of the
viper, and the weaned child shall put his hand on
the cockatrice den; they shall not hurt nor destroy

in all My holy mountain; for the earth shall be full of the knowledge of Jehovah. And in that day there shall be a Root of Jesse, which shall stand for an ensign of the people; to it shall the Gentiles seek, and his rest shall be glorious," chap. xi. 1, 5—10: that these things have not as yet come to pass in any church, much less in the last, is generally allowed. In Jeremiah, " Behold the days come, saith Jehovah, that I will make a new covenant, and this shall be the covenant; I will put My law in in the midst of them, and write it on their hearts, and will be their God, and they shall be My people, and they shall all know Me from the least of them unto the greatest of them," chap. xxxi. 31—34. Rev. xxi. 3: that this prophecy has not been fulfilled in former churches, is also generally acknowledged; the reason was, because they did not approach a visible God, whom all may know, and who is Himself the Word or Law, which He will put in the midst of them, and write on their hearts. Again, in Isaiah, " For JERUSALEM'S sake I will not rest until the righteousness thereof go forth as brightness, and the salvation thereof as a lamp that burneth; and thou shalt be called by a new name, which the mouth of Jehovah shall name; and thou shalt be a CROWN OF GLORY, AND A ROYAL DIADEM in the hand of thy God: Jehovah shall delight in thee, and thy land shall be MARRIED. Behold, thy salvation cometh; behold His reward is with Him: and they shall call them the holy peo-

ple, the Redeemed of Jehovah: and thou shalt be
called, Sought out, a City not forsaken," chap. lxii.
1. to the end.

The future state of this church is also described
at large in the Revelation, which treats of the end
of the former Church, and the rise of the New;
this New Church is described by the New Jerusalem, with all its magnificence, and represented as
the Bride and Wife of the Lamb, chap. xix. 7. xxi.
2, 9. I shall here only transcribe from the Revelation, what is said, when the New Jerusalem was
seen to descend out of heaven: " Behold, the tabernacle of God is with men, and He will dwell
with them, and they shall be His people, and God
Himself shall be with them, and be their God:
and the nations of them which are saved, shall walk
in the light of it: and there shall be no night there.
I Jesus have sent mine angel to testify unto you
these things in the churches. I am the Root and
the Offspring of David, the Bright and Morning
Star: the Spirit and the Bride say, Come; and he
that heareth, let him say, Come; and he that is
athirst, Let him come; and whosoever will, let him
take the water of life freely: Even so, come Lord
Jesus. Amen." (chap. xxi. 2, 24, 25. chap. xxii.
16, 17, 20.)

A COROLLARY.

SHEWING in what the difference between the faith of the old or former Church, and the faith of the New Christian Church principally consists.

THE faith of the former Church teaches, that there have been three divine persons from eternity, each of whom singly, or by himself, is God, as so many creators; but the faith of the New Church teaches, that there is only One Divine Person, consequently only One God, from eternity, and that beside Him there is no other God. The faith of the former Church has therefore maintained, that the Divine Trinity is divided into three persons; but the faith of the New Church maintains, that the Divine Trinity is united in One Person. The faith of the former Church was directed towards a God invisible, unapproachable, with whom there could, be no conjunction, and the idea formed of whom was as of a spirit, which was supposed to be like ether or wind; but the faith of the New Church is directed towards a God visible, approachable, and with whom there is a possibility of conjunction, in whom is the invisible and unapproachable God

as the soul is in the body, and the idea formed of
whom, is that of a Divine Man, because the One
God, who was from eternity, was made man in
time. The faith of the former Church attributes all
power to the invisible God, and denies it to the visible, for it holds that God the Father imputeth faith,
and thereby conferreth eternal life, but that the
visible God only intercedes, and that they both give,
or, according to the Greek Church, God the Father
alone gives, to the Holy Ghost (who is also a God
by Himself, the third in order,) all power of operating the effects of that faith; but the faith of the
New Church attributes to the visible God, in whom
is the invisible, all power of imputing, and also of
operating the effects of salvation. The faith of the
former Church is directed principally towards God
as Creator, and not towards Him as Redeemer and
Saviour at the same time; but the faith of the New
Church is directed towards One God, who is at once
Creator, Redeemer, and Saviour. The faith of the
former Church insisteth, that when faith is once given and imputed, repentance, remission of sins, reno-
vation, regeneration, sanctification, and salvation,
follow of themselves, without any thing of man being mixed or conjoined with them, thus without
his co-operation; but the faith of the New Church
teaches repentance, reformation, regeneration, and
thus the remission of sins by man's co-operation.
The faith of the former Church asserteth the imputation of Christ's merit, as included in the faith so

conferred; but the faith of the New Church teaches an imputation of good and of evil, and of faith at the same time; and that this imputation is agreeable to the Holy Scripture, but the other contrary to it. The former Church maintains the gift of faith, including the merit of Christ, whilst man is as a stock or a stone; it also asserteth a total impotence in spiritual things; but the New Church teaches a faith altogether different, not a faith in the merit of Christ, but in Jesus Christ Himself as God, as Redeemer and Saviour, asserting a freedom of will in man, both to apply himself to reception, and to co-operate with it. The former Church adjoineth charity to its faith as an appendage, but not as possessing any saving efficacy, and thus it forms its religion; but the New Church conjoineth faith in the Lord, and charity towards one's neighbour, as two inseparable things, and so forms its religion: not to mention several other points of disagreement, whence it is evident that, unless a New Church were to be raised up in the place of the old, " NO FLESH COULD BE SAVED, according to the Lord's words in Matt. xxiv. 22.

FINIS.

CPSIA information can be obtained at www.ICGtesting.com
Printed in the USA
BVOW08s2347030315

390215BV00017B/198/P